IRON LOVE

MANIFESTING, ACCEPTING, AND NURTURING TRUE LOVE

Kenyatta Jones-Arietta

Eula Rae Printing & Publishing

Copyright © 2025 by Kenyatta Jones-Arietta

All rights reserved. No part of this publication may be reproduced, distributed, or transmitted in any form or by any means, including photocopying, recording, or other electronic or mechanical methods, without the prior written permission of the publisher, except in the case of brief quotations used in reviews, articles, or scholarly works. For permission requests, please contact:

Eula Rae Printing and Publishing
Rockland County, New York
www.eularae.com

First Edition

ISBN: 978-0-9976748-6-6 Paperback
ISBN: 978-0-9976748-7-3 Hardcover
Library of Congress Control Number: 2025938796

Cover design by Kenyatta Jones-Arietta
Interior design and formatting by Damonza
Printed in the United States of America

Disclaimer:

This book is intended for informational and inspirational purposes only. The author and publisher make no representations or warranties with respect to the accuracy or completeness of the contents and specifically disclaim any implied warranties of fitness for a particular purpose. The content does not replace professional advice in areas such as medical, psychological, legal, or financial matters. The reader is responsible for their own actions, choices, and results. The author and publisher shall not be held liable for any loss or damages incurred in connection with this book.

Publisher's Cataloging-in-Publication Data
Jones-Arietta, Kenyatta.
Iron Love: Manifesting, Accepting, and Nurturing True Love / by Kenyatta Jones-Arietta
p. cm.
Includes bibliographical references.
1. Love—Psychological aspects. 2. Self-actualization. 3. Relationships—Personal growth.
4. Manifestation (New Thought).
ISBN: 978-0-9976748-6-6
Library of Congress Control Number: 2025938796

Dear Lysa:

So glad the Universe connected us. Looking forward to going deeper. Hope you enjoy the journey of From Love.

XO

Author's Note:

While the stories in this book are drawn from my real-life experiences, some names and identifying details have been changed to protect the privacy of those involved.

Table of Contents

Foreword ix
Introduction: The Journey To Iron Love. 1
The Nine Phases Of Iron Love 7
Manifesting Love 13
Recognizing Love. 35
Overcoming Fear 43
Choosing The Path Of Love 59
Committing To Love 71
Incorporating Love. 87
Trusting Love. 101
Supporting Love. 121
Life after Love 133
Staying In Love 143
Acknowledgements. 147

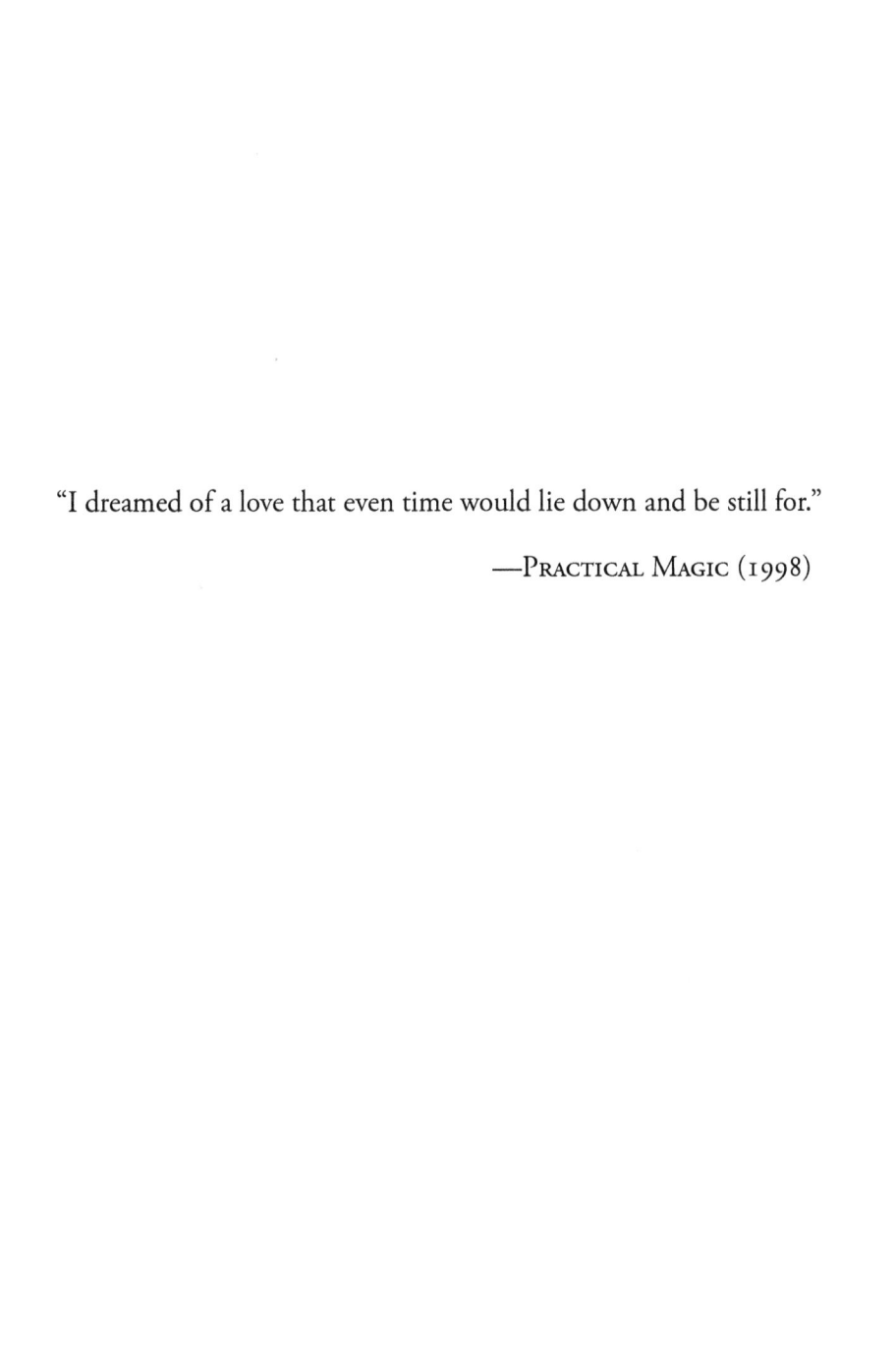

"I dreamed of a love that even time would lie down and be still for."

—Practical Magic (1998)

Foreword

As I reflect on the remarkable journey of my dear friend Kenyatta Jones-Arietta, I am filled with admiration and overcome with joy knowing that by reading this book, you will get a peek into the life and love of this magnificent woman. Over the past quarter-century, she has woven a tapestry of magic that only she could weave. The threads of her life include love, resilience, boundless creativity, perseverance, support of those around her, and a deep knowing that everything is always working out in the Universe.

I wasn't there in the beginning when she and her husband, Rudy of 25 years met, but I've witnessed enough of their relationship to know that the reason behind their success is the never-ending support of each other's growth and dreams. Together, they have not only nurtured a thriving marriage but have also built a life that supports their individual paths to self-actualization. They understand true partnership is rooted in supporting each other's dreams, ambitions, and personal journeys. Their unwavering commitment to each other's growth and the strength of their marriage is the secret to their Iron Love.

Even better, the strength of their relationship has enabled Kenyatta to share and spread her good energy and goodwill with everyone she encounters. I don't care if you are on her real estate team or if you randomly meet her in the subway, her electric *duchenne* smile will pull you in, and she will inspire you. A Duchenne smile is a fancy term psychologists use to describe a genuine smile. You may not know the term, but you know the difference. Kenyatta genuinely cares, is interested, and wants you to do well in life and this shines in her eyes and smile.

In her book, *Iron Love*, Kenyatta invites us into her world—a world where she could have easily ended up as a statistic. Her early life was not easy, and yet she rose above and figured it out. This is where the lesson and inspiration lie for each of us, no matter how dark the night is, if you keep focused forward with an optimistic lens, joy does cometh in the morning.

I have joyfully witnessed her rise, the detours, and bumps in the road, and the resilient spirit in which she rises each morning, determined not just to get through the day, but *from* the day. After meeting her in kickboxing class, her smile pulled me in, and we were instant friends. I remember the day she told me she had to make a choice between opening a healthy fast-food restaurant or starting a real estate business after she achieved her IFBB pro card. She chose real estate.

The beauty of Kenyatta's story isn't in the big leaps but in the small, consistent steps. Her first office was small and above a storefront, a tiny R2M Realty flag hung on the street level, but it was hard to see. The size of the space or the sign didn't matter as much as the giant vision in her heart. From day one, she focused on that small office space, and soon turned it into a larger one on the ground floor on a side street, and then to a premier location on Main Street, which then turned to two locations. She now owns that building, and on the tenth anniversary of R2M, she not only hosted a celebration, she rented a billboard on a major thoroughfare. To say she came a long way from that small sign to the billboard is an understatement.

Not only did her business grow, but she also grew and expanded. Once she got a taste of the universal truth that manifestations follow feelings and beliefs, she was on her way. Through these pages, you will discover not only the milestones and achievements but also the heart and soul poured into every one of her endeavors. I have countless stories I could share about what she has manifested through her deep knowing and focused beliefs, but I will suffice to say, what has worked in her life can also work for you. The universal energy that seems to follow her and be at her disposal is there for you, too. So while her story will captivate you, the lessons are woven throughout for you to try on and prove to yourself that what you focus on grows and manifests.

Kenyatta's story is not just about building a life but about crafting a legacy of love, leadership, and limitless possibilities. Nothing is impossible when you believe and back up your beliefs with consistent actions.

Join me in celebrating a life well-lived and a future filled with promise and her and Rudy's Iron Love. May her life inspire and empower you as it has inspired me.

With love and admiration for all you are in my life,
Michele Phillips, Award Winning Author of *Happiness is a Habit*, Speaker and Workshop Leader

Introduction

The Journey to Iron Love

During my formative years, I didn't have the kind of parental guidance I suspect many people do. My mother was busy navigating her own life, which was complex and messy at times. Her ex-husband, Ralph; my half-brother's father (and namesake) left the family home before we could grasp what having a father meant.

While our mother worked to better her situation, Ralph and I were placed in the care of Eula and Robert Jones (our mother's adoptive parents; our grandparents). They did their best to provide stability and Christian upbringing, but life had other plans for us.

My world changed forever when Eula, the woman who had been my anchor, passed away three days after my 17th birthday and three days before her 73rd. Her death left Ralph and I with a grandfather and mother too broken to care for us. To make matters even more challenging, I was three months pregnant, and my "baby daddy" had just been sentenced to five years in prison.

As for my own father, after spending my childhood believing my brother and I shared the same dad, thanks to a slip from my grandfather's lip I found out that was not the case.

I recall waiting for my mother to arrive from work, the back of my legs sticking to the plastic-wrapped floral wingback chair in my grandparents living room, where I sat directly facing the front door. As she stepped inside, I confronted her, "Granddaddy says I look like my daddy. I don't look like Ralph. What gives?"

After a bit of explaining, she finally gave me a name: Norman Harold Peoples, though most people called him Harold.

I called every Norman or N.H. Peoples listed in the White Pages, asking, **"Are You My Father?"**—like a real-life version of the Dr. Suess classic. I picked up the receiver and rotated the dial, number after number on my grandparents' old rotary phone. By the age of 11, I had become a master at cold calling.

I didn't meet my father until I was 14. He passed away when I was 21. But in those seven short years, we spent quite a bit of time getting to know each other. Harold was a gentle giant—tall, stocky, kind of like James Avery from *The Fresh Prince of Bel-Air*, only with lighter skin and a longer, curlier horseshoe of hair. He wore a Cheshire Cat smile, especially when he looked at my mother. I loved my dad, and he loved me too. He was my lion—just not with a full mane.

I didn't connect it until years after his passing, but if Harold was an animal, he would have been the perfect blend of Mufasa from *The Lion King* and Lion from the 1978 movie, *The Wiz*. He was as strong as he was silly… at least to me. Decades later, I discovered my dad was NOT my biological father. (I always wondered why my mother liked the Jerry Springer show.) That revelation unraveled yet another layer of my identity, leaving me with more questions than answers.

Imagine being almost 50 years old and erasing half of your family tree with nothing more than an unexpected DNA match as the only clue to your true identity.

Back to the drawing board.

Yet, if life has taught me anything, it's that even the hardest truths have a way of shaping us for the better—everything is in divine order.

At age 17, without a solid support system after grandma's passing, I still managed to get myself on the DDOT bus every morning, traveling across town to school. Rain, sleet, hail, snow—it didn't matter. With my baby girl, Tiera strapped to my chest in an infant carrier, I shuffled through it all. I found comfort in the routine. It offered a sense of stability during an otherwise chaotic time.

My mother had me transferred from Osborn High to Booth Memorial when she found out I was pregnant. Booth was a school for teen moms that offered a nursery where caregivers looked after the students' infants and toddlers while they studied. We were able to go down to feed our babies whenever we needed to, and otherwise we learned not only math, reading, and writing, but were also taught parenting basics like feeding schedules, diaper changing and nursing. Still, there were countless lessons I had to learn on my own—child rearing, money management, resilience, relationships. With life as my teacher, I managed to figure things out, one challenge at a time.

At 17, I relied on public assistance and worked as a dancer in strip clubs in and around Detroit to make ends meet. I took on the stage name *Angel*, inspired by the character from the 1984 American exploitation thriller of the same name. Student by day—pursuing a business degree at Marygrove College on the city's Northwest side after graduating high school early—and entertainer by night. It wasn't easy, but even then, I knew I wanted more for myself and my little girl.

In the waning months of my 19th year, I decided to take a leap-of-faith move to New York City. Sinatra sang it best: "*If I can make it there, I'll make it anywhere...*" My first stop was Flashdancers, a strip club on 52nd and Broadway, where I entertained in the evening, working there to pay the bills while pursuing a modeling career during the day. I was represented by Grace Del Marco, a Black-owned and operated agency located in the Empire State Building.

A chance connection through my dad Harold led me to a great-aunt (his aunt) who lived in Bed-Stuy. I stayed with her in her one-bedroom apartment for a few months before landing my own flat in Hell's Kitchen. My new digs were secured with the help of Rob, a disc jockey at Flash, and the principal broker of R.J. Douglas Realty, a small real estate office in midtown Manhattan. This marked the beginning of my real estate journey.

Not only did Rob spin my favorite R&B tunes—he also encouraged me to get my real estate license and became my first sponsor. While real estate wasn't a perfect fit for me at that time, it planted a seed that would later take root and grow beyond my wildest dreams.

After months of pounding the pavement, dripping in sweat and adding calluses to my already flattened feet, I earned my first commission check for a tenant-represented rental transaction… and back to the club I went. The money at Flashdancers was just too good to walk away from. It was like *flypaper*, and I was a fly.

I lost myself in the hustle for a few years—working to eat, pay the bills, go on go-sees and then head to a club, eventually exploring New York City's other premier clubs—Scores, Stringfellow's, The Gold Nugget. Though the scenery changed, it was all the same. It began to feel like a never-ending hamster wheel, like living *Groundhog Day* starring me instead of Bill Murray.

Though I landed some cool gigs—doing the first *Sony PlayStation* commercial, music videos, product ads, and extra work on *The City* (a daytime soap spinoff of *Loving*) and TV shows like *Law and Order*, it was evident that I wasn't going to be the next supermodel. Eventually, I decided it was time to go in a different direction. I enrolled in the New York School of Interior Design (NYSID), earning my AAS degree in 2000—the same year Rudy and I married. Our *courtship* was brief, having met in spring of 1999.

Rudy proposed to me eight months after we met. The proposal was as down to Earth as we have always been. There were no public or grand gestures, no holiday, or seasonal themes to tie into. In fact, I had just woken up from a nap, snuggling with my Tiera. I was wiping the crust out of my eyes, yawning, trying to process what was going on when Rudy asked me to marry him. I was so surprised, I almost forgot to respond. "Yes! Yes! Yes!" I finally answered after he nervously looked at me and said, "You haven't said yes yet."

> **Fun fact:**
>
> *Rudy's family roots trace back to Michigan—his maternal grandmother was born just outside of Detroit, not far from where I lived during my early teens. I often tease that I came all the way to New York to meet and marry a man whose roots were practically in my backyard.*

That same year, I moved to the suburbs with Rudy and Tiera in tow—kicking and screaming. (For clarification, I was the one kicking and screaming.) I embarked on a reverse commute to Manhattan for six years, working as an interior designer/furniture salesperson. After a series of unmistakable signs from the Universe—including a *"life is too short"* wake-up call, delivered through the tragic loss of a dear friend—I decided to give real estate another shot. In the grand scheme of things, I had nothing to lose.

By 2006, Rudy and I had given Tiera two beautiful—now not-so-little— brothers, Rudy and Sean. Postpartum, I began a fitness journey that opened the door to the world of bodybuilding. What started out as a goal to fit back into a size 6 (from a size 20) evolved into a complete lifestyle change.

Rudy and I trained and competed for several years. I even won my IFBB pro card in 2012 and became a sponsored athlete for BNRG (Bio-Nutritional Research Group), the makers of Power Crunch Protein. Those years taught me discipline, focus, and the power of perseverance—qualities that would later help me build R2M Realty, Inc. the multimillion-dollar real estate brokerage I created, own, and manage today.

And then, there came *Iron Love*. The book you're reading right now.

I have been writing ever since I was old enough to string words into phrases. Who could have known then that it was prepping me for the day I would be called to share my life and *Iron Love* journey with you. One evening, while listening to *Having It All* by John Assaraf, the words to *Iron Love* began to build up in my mind like a shaken can of soda ready to explode.

I couldn't ignore the urge to write them out. I paused the audiobook, put my earbuds in the case on the nightstand, opened up the Notes app on my mobile phone, and began downloading. I tapped on my phone well into the night, yawning and squinting until I drifted off to sleep. By morning, I realized I wasn't just writing a book—I was sharing the story of my life, my love, and the lessons I've learned.

I am not a relationship expert by any means. Nope, I'm not a love doctor—there is no *PH. D* behind my name. In fact, I am the first to admit that I am an infinite *student* of love and life. But after 52+ years on this planet, I've learned one undeniable truth: **What you put out into the Universe, you get back, and that includes love.**

Love is an energy, a feeling, a way of living and perceiving life. Love can apply to an intimate relationship with a domestic partner, or a deep connection with a parent, child, friend, or even a pet. The concept of *Iron Love* came to me back in 2013 when Rudy and I were immersed in bodybuilding culture. It began as a *Facebook* page I created to celebrate strong, committed, and enduring relationships—relationships that, much like iron, were forged through fire, pressure, and time. Inspired by couples I admired, I wanted to share their secrets with a world that seemed to be filled with so many people searching for love or fighting to hold on to the love they had. Once upon a time, *I* was one of those searching souls.

Iron Love is the culmination of my experiences—the struggles, the triumphs, and the little life nuggets I've accumulated along the way. Whether you're searching for love, learning to nurture it, or figuring out how to hold on to it, my hope is that this book will serve as a guide. A testament to the idea that love, in its truest form, is built to last.

The Nine Phases of Iron Love

Throughout my life's journey, I've identified nine phases necessary to attract, build and sustain iron love—a love that is strong, enduring, and transformative.

Each chapter will guide you through these phases, offering insights and strategies I hope will help you find, cultivate and maintain meaningful love in your life.

1. **Manifesting Love.** Before the right love can enter your life, you must first understand what you are welcoming. Creating a clear mental picture of the love you seek helps remove obstacles and aligns you with the energy needed to attract it.

2. **Recognizing Love.** The clarity with which you define and manifest your iron love determines how easy it will be to recognize it when it appears. When certain characteristics are left undefined, love can be harder to see, potentially causing us to overlook what is meant for us.

    This chapter includes a bonus section: **Overcoming Fear.**

    Fear is often the main culprit behind our inability to recognize what's truly meant for us. Even when we recognize love, fear and deeply ingrained limiting beliefs—often shaped by past experiences or generational trauma—can prevent us from fully embracing it.

3. **Choosing the Path of Love (Accepting Love)**. Manifesting and recognizing love are only the beginning; the next step is accepting it with an open and vulnerable heart. In order for the path to open fully, your partner must also choose the path with you. This is where you no longer walk alone.

4. **Committing to Love.** Love requires commitment (from both partners) in order for it to grow, deepen, and form a strong foundation. Like building muscle through consistent weight training, iron love gets stronger through daily effort, intentionality, and unwavering dedication.

5. **Incorporating Love**. True commitment to love doesn't mean losing yourself; rather, it means integrating love into your life in a way that complements and enhances who you are. This phase focuses on maintaining individuality while fostering unity.

6. **Trusting Love.** Trust is the cornerstone of love. It can be tested over time and, when reinforced, becomes unshakable. Without trust, love lacks a solid foundation on which to build from.

7. **Supporting Love**. Explore what it means to stand firm in the face of life's most daunting challenges. Love is easy in moments of joy, but its true strength is revealed in the moments that test our very survival. This chapter delves into the kind of love that holds steady through fear, pain, and the unknown—the love that carries us through battles we never expected to fight and forces us to confront our deepest vulnerabilities.

8. **Life After Love.** Whether through loss, separation, or a natural ending, love sometimes reaches a conclusion. This phase explores how to heal, grow, and learn to love again—restarting the cycle with renewed wisdom and an open heart.

9. **Staying in Love.** Sustaining love required continuous nurturing, growth, and a shared dedication to deepening the connection over time.

Through stories and experiences shared, each chapter of this book will offer guidance on navigating each phase with intention and resilience, helping you cultivate an iron love that endures and evolves through life's inevitable shifts and challenges.

I Loved You First

I loved you first: but afterwards your love

Outsoaring mine, sang such a loftier song

As I drowned the friendly cooing of my dove.

Which owes the other most? My love was long,

And yours one moment seemed to was more strong;

I loved and guessed at you, you construed me

And loved me for what might or might not be-

Nay, weights and measures do us both a wrong.

For verily love knows not 'mine' or 'thine':

With separate 'I' and 'thou' free love has done,

For one is both and both are one in love:

Rich love knows nought of 'thine that is not mine;'

Both have the strength, and both have the length thereof,

Both of us, of the love which makes us one.

-Christina Rossetti

Rudy and I: In The Beginning

"I'm only going to make about $50,000 a year," Rudy said, intent on not breaking eye contact as we stood in front of the floating shelves in my bedroom, discussing our impending future together. He wore a loose-fitting white short-sleeved polo with a pair of semi-wrinkled khakis that seemed to be one size too big. Despite his lean frame, he was toned, with veins running down his arms like channels in a river.

His declaration was a bit of a pill to swallow, since I'd recently only dated and been pursued by older, well-established men. But there I stood in certainty. "Okay," I replied, having no idea what the future held but affirming that this 24-year-old human was to be my life partner. I knew we were destined to ride this rollercoaster we call life together—for as long as the Universe would have it be.

Now before you say *"Fifty thousand dollars? What's wrong with that?"* you must know that we were living in New York City, an island where the cost of living was about a 95% higher cost of living than the U.S. national average. In fact, it was nearly double what it cost to live in my hometown, Detroit.

I am also three and a half years older than Rudy—though when we met, I could have sworn he told me he was 28. To this day, Rudy will tell you that I heard what I wanted to hear. But I now know that I heard what I *needed* to hear.

Rudy and I met at Lace in Rockland County, NY, a strip club I worked at back in 1999. It was right before the Y2K panic, and kind of like the Rihanna song, *"We Found Love in a Hopeless Place."* In addition to the immediate physical attraction, we just clicked. We could talk about anything, and we conversed about everything. But when I realized his age, I pulled away. He was so fresh out of college, the ink on his diploma was probably still drying. We started out as friends with benefits—yes, both the friendship and the benefits were real. And even now, Rudy is still the best friend I could have ever hoped for or dreamed of.

At that time, I *couldn't see* how Rudy could be the one for me. So, I did what seemed logical at the time: I tried to get him to date other people. I mean, there just was no way possible this kid could be my forever person.

Iron Love

But then it happened…

Rudy and I had been hanging out for almost six months when he was planning to go out on a date with someone else. The thought of him connecting with another person was enough to wake me up. I mean, if he seriously started dating another woman, I couldn't see her being ok with our special friendship. The possibility of losing him was real, hitting me like a ton of bricks. I knew I had a decision to make.

What we shared was just too good to risk not having nor finding again. I had to take a chance. Up to this point Rudy and I spent quite a bit of time together. We ventured out to different restaurants, caught movies, strolled through the city parks and squares, explored architecture, and visited museums. I loved analyzing and critiquing public spaces—things like lighting and seating plans. I enjoyed listening to music, dancing, trying new foods, you name it. Rudy was the person I could do it all with.

And to this day, with all the changes in our lives over the past 25 years, the one thing that has remained constant is that Rudy Arietta is still my person.

Aside from being the youngest person I'd ever dated, Rudy didn't come packaged as Prince Charming. He had an incredible physique, was fun to hang with, and amazing in bed. But he wasn't the sharpest dresser. And at 24, he was already balding and had horrible acne. (Of course, that clean head of his is now one of the hottest things about him). But let's back up a bit. How did we go from him planning to go out with someone else to the $50,000 declaration?

This is where our story begins.

MANIFESTING LOVE

If you are reading this book, it is most likely because you desire the ultimate love in your life, want to grow your current relationship, or maybe you're questioning whether the relationship you're in is the right one for you. My hope is that the stories and experiences shared in *Iron Love* will assist you in manifesting, recognizing, and sustaining the love that you've been longing for—within yourself and with others.

Let's begin with manifesting. To manifest something is to bring it into existence, turning something from an idea into reality. I, my friend, am here to tell you that YOU have the ability to manifest the love and life that you want. One tool you can use to help you with manifesting is *creative visualization*.

Creative visualization is more than just imagining a goal. It's about actively engaging your senses to make the experience *feel* real. In a 2023 article "The Science Behind Creative Visualization" published by *Inner Growth Coach*, this work explains how visualization activates the same neural pathways as physically performing the actions, effectively priming your mind and body for success. By repeatedly practicing visualization, you create a mental rehearsal that not only boosts confidence but also aligns your subconscious with your goals.

Similarly, a 2022 *Askdifference.com* article by Fiza Rafique, "Manifestation vs. Visualization—What's the Difference?" highlights that while both practices are powerful on their own, they are most effective when used together.

Visualization provides the clarity and focus necessary to manifest desires by allowing you to feel and act as though the outcome is already happening.

Broken down, creative visualization is being able to act and feel as though the desired result has already been achieved. Imagine what it would feel like to be in that ultimate love relationship—what your days together would look like, the emotions you'd experience, the shared moments of joy. Tap into your innermost desires, and mentally move forward as if it's already happening. *Feel* the love and joy you want inside you. It's kind of like the old saying, "Fake it until you make it." By creating the feeling that something has already occurred, you can attract it into your life.

When you feel love, you give off a different energy, which is felt by all who encounter you. For example, have you ever found yourself single for a while with no prospects in sight, and then you're in a relationship, and all of a sudden it seems that everyone else is *now* interested? That is due in part to the love energy that you have begun to emit.

You can use creative visualization not only to manifest love but to bring about anything you want to attract to your life. Athletes, for example, often use creative visualization to achieve peak performance. The 2021 *Very Well Fit* article by Elizabeth Quinn "How Imagery and Visualization Can Improve Athletic Performance" shares that many elite athletes mentally rehearse their routines, visualizing every movement and success before they step onto the field or stage. Their vivid imagery enhances focus, reduces anxiety, and primes their bodies for action. Similarly, when manifesting love, picturing your ideal relationship creates emotional alignment that helps attract it into your life.

But visualization isn't just about seeing the outcome—it's also about the emotions behind it. As world-renowned mindset and performance expert John Assaraf so brilliantly puts it in his audio program, *Winning the Game of Money*, "The emotions you feel are the attractors in your life, not your circumstances." The feelings you generate while visualizing, such as joy, gratitude, or excitement, are what create the magnetic pull that draws your desires closer to you. In other words, it all begins with how you feel and the energy you project into the world around you.

"How do I know this works?", you ask. Well, because it works for me. And if there is one thing that I've learned for certain on this life journey, it's that I'm not special. I don't deserve, nor am I entitled to any more than anyone else. My sole advantage is that I've learned to follow the signs the Universe lays out for me. Through trial and error, I have become what I like to call a *master manifester*.

I first became aware of the concept of manifesting through a book titled *Creative Visualization* by Shakti Gawain. I was drawn to the work displayed at a bookstore in midtown Manhattan more than 30 years ago. (How can it possibly be that long ago?) However, it wasn't until early 1999 that I applied the visualizing/manifesting principles in an exercise to write the recipe for my iron love.

I was living in South Ozone Park, Queens at the time, and I'd grown extremely frustrated with dating. My love relationships all seemed to wax and wane for about two years before fizzling out. Looking back, with the exception of a few anomalies, I can see that I had formed a *habit*... I attracted and was attracted to the same type of person and engaged in similar experiences over and over again. For the most part my love interests were brilliant but emotionally unavailable, with intimacy issues and strained relationships with their mothers.

It wasn't until after my last breakup that I had gotten to the point where I was finally able to recognize the pattern and decided enough was enough. I was ready for something different. I remember sitting on the porch of the duplex I rented, puffing on a Dunhill Blue, when the thought hit me. I inhaled, *What am I doing?* And exhaled, *Why do I choose to be in relationships with guys who can't commit?* (Because being and staying in any relationship is a choice*).*

I inhaled again, flaring the cherry at the tip of my cigarette, sending a smoke signal into the heavens above. My eyes watered, though I'm not entirely sure if it was due to the cloud emitting from my tobacco stick or the tears beginning to form in my eyes as I reflected on my romantic misfortune. I pressed the butt into the concrete walkway, twisting it into the ground to extinguish its light, and I made a conscious decision, *I'm going to* **manifes***t my life partner.*

I didn't remember Gawain's book at that time. In fact, I didn't recall *Creative Visualization* until doing a preliminary interview with communications expert Patricia Stark when I began writing *Iron Love*, but its principles were about to be evoked into my life all the same. *If not Gawain's work, where did I get the idea to write out the description of my ideal partner? How did I think to try manifesting?* You ask. Believe it or not, the answer is *Practical Magic.*

Practical Magic, a contemporary fantasy novel written by American novelist Alice Hoffman, adapted to the 1998 romantic fantasy starring Sandra Bullock (as Sally Owens) and Nicole Kidman (as her saucy sister, Gillian). In the movie, Sally and Gillian were born into a long bloodline of witches who lived in the same small town for generations. The sisters are frequently teased and ridiculed by the locals, who, driven by superstition, both fear and scorn the family's magical lineage.

Aside from being quirky, social misfits, the family was cursed. If any of the Owens women fell in love, the man she gave her heart to would be doomed to die, leaving the Owens descendent heartbroken and alone. In order to avoid the devastating fate, Sally decided to wish for a guy whose qualities and characteristics couldn't possibly exist. This way she could never fall in love… that was, until the day the aberration came knocking on her door. I won't give any more details just in case you decide to check it out for yourself. I've watched it more than a half dozen times over the years—most recently with my granddaughter… it may be a wee bit dated now, but it's still rather entertaining.

After setting my intention to manifest my life partner, I went inside to grab a Uniball, a piece of vellum, and a hardcover book to write on top of. As a design student, I wrote everything on vellum. I then ventured back out and sat with Tiera under the stars. She was nine at the time. I focused on what I really wanted in a partner. I wrote:

Send me someone that:

- Supports me in my endeavors.
- Someone that's not afraid to love me.
- Someone I can share and enjoy life with.
- Someone that will love Tiera.
- Someone I can build a family empire with.
- Someone creative that loves and appreciates art and music.

- Someone who is good at and enjoys sex.
- Someone who is as, if not more, ambitious than I am.
- Someone that is sensitive yet powerful.
- Someone I can learn from and grow with.
- Someone who doesn't smother me.
- Someone who gives me enough yet leaves me wanting more.

I folded the prescription into what looked like a neat piece of flattened origami and placed it under an ivory pillar candle on the top shelf of the wall-hung shelving system in the bedroom I shared with Tiera. The room was large and bright with lots of windows, high ceilings, and enough space for both my queen bed and Tiera's twin.

The beds were positioned across from each other like pieces set on a chess board ready for action. But unlike opposing sides poised for battle, Tiera and I often slept snuggled together, enveloped in the sheer canopy of my four-poster wrought iron bed. There has never been anything more comforting than a good snuggle fest.

The words I wrote that fateful evening lay pressed together in silence, hidden beneath the candle. The paper clung to itself, holding the words close, awaiting the day I would discover it again. The revelation came during our move from Queens to Rockland County.

While packing, I lifted the pillar from the shelf where it sat, smiling as the marquise-cut diamond ring on my finger caught the brilliant sunlight streaming in from the bedroom window. It was then that I saw it—a forgotten piece of paper. I picked it up and gently unfolded it to reveal my vision of love. After reading it, I turned to Rudy, who was catching his breath from moving a box out to the U-Haul.

"This is you!" I held up the paper for him to see. That was the moment I realized my desires had become a reality… Our reality.

∽

When I mentally committed to writing *Iron Love*, I shared my relationship manifesting experience with a friend of mine, Lucia. Full of excitement she said, "Oh my God! Did I ever tell you how Sid and I met?"

"No", I responded. I couldn't wait to hear their story.

Lucia went on to tell me about some horrible guy she dated before Sid that her friends hated for her. "Well," she went on, "After we broke up, while on a train to Long Island, one of my girlfriends suggested that we write down what we wanted in a partner, along with the date and time that we would meet. Our other friend couldn't be bothered, but I decided to go for it. I wrote out a date and time." Lucia continued, "Sid and I met briefly that February, though we didn't initially remember it, but when we went on our first date, it was the exact day and time that I projected!" That was 15 years ago, and the pair are still going strong.

You may be thinking that Lucia knew the day and time she wrote, and so she asked Sid out to correspond with what she'd written. But she didn't ask him out. Sid asked Lucia out and he did not know about her penned desire. That, my friend, is literally how the Universe works. It can be that simple.

In *Having It All*, Assaraf shares that he too manifested his wife, Maria in the exact same way I manifested my iron love. John wrote out a detailed vision of the qualities he wanted in a life partner, focusing on values and interests, and the Universe delivered.

Our stories of manifesting love aren't the only magical love stories out there, but through sharing our experiences, I hope that you will be encouraged to attract the partner of your dreams. You deserve to be happy. And you deserve to experience true love.

∽

Ready to manifest your Iron Love?

Find somewhere to sit (preferably alone) and really tap into YOU (Your thoughts. Your desires). Concentrate on embracing love. What does that feel like to you? Holding on to that vibe, ask yourself, what are the characteristics you desire in a significant other? You can tap the description out in the notes app on your phone or use your laptop to type them out, but in my opinion, good old-fashioned writing is the best and most effective method to use for manifesting. Putting pen to paper, letting your ideas flow from your brain receptors, through your body, down your arm, to the palm of your hand, into your fingers, then poured out onto paper is pure magic.

No matter which way you choose to cast your projection, just get it out and let it go. Don't dwell on it and don't worry. Worry is like praying for your desires not to become reality and dwelling on it only *stirs the pot* of manifestation. *Stirring the pot* creates momentum which causes a vortex. When it comes to manifesting, we're not interested in whirlpools. We want to create clear paths.

And by all means, don't try looking for it. Let me tell you, had I tried looking for my iron love, I would never have found him. He was EXACTLY what I wrote I wanted, but the things that I didn't write came in ways I would not have imagined.

I didn't define *how old* my ideal partner would be. I hadn't added any physical characteristics. I didn't say how much money he would make a year. In fact, what I wrote was that I wanted "someone I could *build* an empire with." The things I didn't define were left to be interpreted by the Universe and the Universe did not disappoint.

When it comes to love and achieving other goals no matter the size or category, manifesting is an extremely important and powerful tool. Manifesting by way of writing out what it is you want assists in giving you the clearest picture as to what that desire actually is. If you don't have a visual, how do you know if and when you achieve it? If you don't have an idea what love is to you, how will you recognize it? If you don't set a destination, how will you know when you've arrived?

Be sure to focus on the characteristics and personality traits, and not a specific person when defining and visualizing your ideal love relationship. In *Creative Visualization*, Gawain notes, "This technique cannot be used to control the behavior of others or to cause them to do something against their will." Trust me, I've tried. And to this day, I am beyond grateful that that's not the way the Universe works.

The effect of creative visualization "is to dissolve our internal barriers to natural harmony and self-realization allowing everyone to manifest in his or her most positive aspect," Gawain advises.

In a 2007 interview with self-help author Steve Pavlina, John Assaraf shared, "We become, have, and attract what we think about and act upon *correctly* the most." *Correctly* being the key word here. Too often people *say* they want to experience a special loving relationship, or attempt to manifest love, but at the same time, hold on to those limiting beliefs, they secretly fear their dreams won't come true.

Having one foot in faith and the other in fear or doubt pretty much cancels out one another, leaving your desire to remain unfulfilled and your feet stuck where they stand. Remember the vortex I mentioned earlier? Moving in an endless circle. Neither scenario leads you *forward* or closer to your hopes and dreams—different struggles, yet producing the same undesired result.

Faith is imperative when manifesting. You must have faith and know you weren't put on this planet to be unhappy. You chose to come here to experience life as a human being and to know and feel love, joy and happiness.

During the 2023 *An Illuminated Life* workshop I attended at the Omega Institute in Rhinebeck, NY facilitated by *New York Times* best-selling author and psychic medium, Laura Lynne Jackson, Jackson shared that life is a collective lesson in love. Whether it's love with self or a significant other, love with family and friends, love with your children, even love for/from your pet, experiencing love is ultimately what life is all about.

That's not to say that love is all you should experience. Negative and unexpected things can happen, and they will. It's all a part of the journey. Think about it, if you never experienced the cold rain and clouds, you wouldn't fully appreciate the warm sunshine as much now, would you? Not to mention, storms help with facilitating growth... trees, plants, and even people.

The question becomes do you *choose* to sit inside, moping about something you cannot control? Or do you grab your rain coat, boots, and an umbrella and go dance in the rain? That storm won't last forever. Between you and I, I'd much rather leave the rain gear behind, and just go for it. (Though my hair may protest.)

On to manifesting. It is crucial that our minds and spirits are aligned in order for the exercise of manifesting to work. When you visualize being with your iron love, concentrate on feeling the love that the relationship brings into your life and move forward in faith, knowing that your love is already on its way. The seeds of love have been planted and the roots are forming even though you can't physically see them.

Moving forward in faith means trusting that your desires have already been set into motion, even though you may not yet have physical proof.

Speaking of seeds, farmers, experts in the art of nurturing growth, sow seeds all the time. Farmers are also among the greatest practitioners of faith. Farmers bury seeds in the ground, water the earth and make sure they receive ample sunlight, to nourish the hidden life within. They don't unearth them to check for root hairs or signs of sprouting. Instead, they trust the process, knowing from experience that as long as they do *their part*, the earth will bear fruit. In many ways, the *faith* employed to grow a garden is quite like the *vehicle* of manifesting. A vehicle that you use to get you from:

A. Your imagination

to

B. Your reality

But if you don't know how to drive the vehicle or if you don't believe that you are capable of operating it, that vehicle is not going to get you very far. You have to believe that you have the *key* to start the engine; the personal power to use it and know that you are worthy and deserving of reaching your desired destination.

A practice you can use to help you get into the right mindset to begin manifesting the life and iron love you desire is to employ daily *affirmations*. Affirmations are positive statements that can assist you in overcoming negative thoughts and limiting beliefs. Following is a list of some of my favorite affirmations:

- I am worthy of love.
- I love myself.
- I am deserving of a partner who loves and respects me.
- I am powerful.

- I am worthy of happiness.
- I am surrounded by positive and loving beings.
- I am surrounded by love.
- Love and happiness flow through me.
- I have the power to create the reality of my dreams.
- I am confident and strong.
- I attract the right people.
- I have an abundance of love and joy in my life.
- My dreams manifest into reality.
- I have a happy and loving relationship with myself and others.
- I am more than enough.

Try some of these on for size or create a list of your own. Modify them to match your desired goal. Write your affirmations out and repeat them one or more times a day.

Ideally, the best times to practice this exercise are in the morning before you begin your day and in the evening when you start to wind down, though you can do this exercise anytime. I'm more for morning manifesting myself, though I do also employ this practice some evenings as well, depending on my schedule. In addition, I like posting my affirmations on the mirror above my vanity so I can see them when I'm getting ready for the day.

With every goal you are able to realize, you gain the confidence to manifest something bigger; something greater—possibilities are limited only by your imagination. And don't forget the power of *thankfulness* and *gratitude*. It is extremely important to water your dreams and desires with thankfulness, even before they have been fulfilled.

Acknowledge what you already have, and express gratitude for every blessing, big or small. When we don't give thanks for what we've received—life, love, shelter, or any other gift—it's almost like shunning the very source that makes miracles possible.

I remember when this epiphany hit. We were living in an early 1920's three-bedroom Colonial in Tappan, NY. It was the cutest little house we had just about outgrown. I was frustrated that there wasn't enough space to put things—the toys, the clothes, the luggage. Just when I thought we had it all figured out, converting the attic into additional living space, our daughter moved back home… with a baby.

With the *perceived* tightness in our quarters, I was constantly in a bad mood, focused on what we didn't have or what we still needed. Then one day, while digging through the top drawer of my pedestal file, I came across a Tiffany blue matte leather pouch I nearly forgot about. Inside was a magnificent set of clear crystal rosary beads, finished with a sterling silver crucifix. They'd been given to me by my late client, Buddy Higgins, before he passed several years prior. I had been hired to help him sell his family home when he was diagnosed with cancer.

Not being Catholic, I had no idea what I was supposed to do with them, but being a religious article, it didn't feel right to dispose of them, so I put them in the drawer. That day, while looking for a pair of scissors, I noticed the soft colored bag. I took the beads out, held them up, and started fidgeting with them. Something about holding them seemed to give me a sense of calm. *Interesting*, I thought. I brought them upstairs to our bedroom and placed them on my side of the bed.

The next morning, I woke around 6am. Rudy had already left to hit the gym before work. I laid in bed, tucked under the covers with my face barely peeking out. I stared at the beads. I picked them up and held them in my hand. Starting with the cross, I held the strand in hand and said aloud: *I am grateful and thankful for this new day.* Then, one by one, I rolled each bead between my pointer finger and thumb, reflecting on all the wonderful things that make up my life. I called each one out loud.

I don't know what prompted me to do it. I just did. It soon became a habit—the thing I did immediately after listening to a John Assaraf meditation. With this new practice, I began focusing on how blessed I was to have a house at all, let alone a home filled with warmth and love.

My childhood dream had come true and I hadn't even noticed. I'd been so consumed with focusing on what we didn't have that I failed to see that everything I always wanted was what I already had. The feel-good energy that generated from that realization was as transformative as Dorothy clicking her heels three times and being back in Kansas. Before we knew it, there was no place like our new home, with all the space we needed. It was as though our appreciation for what we had opened the door for what we wanted. And that is where we remain to this day, still extremely grateful and thankful.

If you happen to find yourself in the rut of focusing on what you don't have, give gratitude a try. Initially, it may be challenging to come up with things to be thankful for, but the more you practice it, the more you realize just how blessed you really are. Eyesight—the ability to see these words on the page (or hear them), the ability to feel, a sound mind and body... none of it is guaranteed. Acknowledging your blessings is one of the most powerful ways to unlock the door for more.

Now, back to manifesting. Let's begin with something simple—visualize yourself out on a dance floor having a good time. With that in mind, act on it. Phone a few friends and make plans to go dancing. Oh yes! A bit of action ***IS*** required in manifesting. I don't want to give the impression that all you have to do is think about what you want. In this scenario, you actually have to get dressed, go out, and bust a move.

Manifesting really can be that simple. Unless you decide to engage with prospects using a dating app, getting out and connecting with others is still one of the best ways to meet new people. You may not initially meet your iron love, but maybe you meet someone who eventually introduces you to them. You'll never know unless you take those first steps.

Take our farmer; he doesn't just look at the field and hope that corn will be ready for harvest in the fall. He understands that a bountiful crop requires *action*. He must till the ground, fertilize the soil, plant the seeds, and nurture the budding stalks before reaping the fruits of his labor. Or let's consider bodybuilders—they eat right and workout consistently knowing their actions will produce their desired results. They don't just stare at themselves in the mirror and hope... with a cookie in hand.

Over the years of bodybuilding and selling real estate, I've heard countless people declare things they want to manifest in their lives—the seeds they wish to plant and see bear fruit. I've also witnessed many of them *self-sabotage*, allowing the strangling weeds of worry to take root—coming up with every possible reason why it won't work. And as a result, their predictions become self-fulfilling, and their desires wither before they can bloom. Instead of providing water and sunlight to nurture their seeds, they cast a dark cloud over their field of dreams, depriving it of the nutrients needed to grow. Don't do it.

❦

Utilizing the practice of manifesting, my iron love and I have brought countless things to life. From realizing our dream home—which at one point graced both of our vision boards—to unforgettable vacations, investments, thriving careers, the completion of Rudy's dissertation, and even the realization of this very book you're holding in your hands now (or listening to)... manifestation and gratitude have been key components of our journey.

Among these incredible moments, aside from manifesting my life partner, one of my favorite stories of manifesting is earning my *International Federation of Bodybuilding (IFBB)* figure pro card—a dream realized through focus, determination, and a gentle nudge from a friend.

Bodybuilding was my and Rudy's world from 2009 until the end of 2013. As for manifesting the pro card win, it was the summer of 2012. I pinned a replica of an IFBB pro card onto the gold gilt framed vision board mounted on the wall in our home office. The card itself was a credit card sized, stock paper license received after winning an *NPC (National Physique Committee) National* competition.

As a figure competitor, when you win your pro card, you are presented with a trophy topped with a bikini clad figurine, or presented with a gold medal, hung from a red, white, and blue patriotic ribbon, all in front of an auditorium filled with spectators. The pro card itself is received via U.S. post a few weeks later.

To assist in visualizing the pro card win, I didn't just write out "I achieved the IFBB pro card." I downloaded a photo of a card, whited-out the name of the athlete originally printed on it, along with the year it was issued. This, of course, was in addition to working out and eating right.

I photocopied the newly edited version, filled in the current year, 2012, and typed in my full name. Then, before mounting it to my board, I sat and intentionally created the feeling of what it would be like to actually sign my own real pro card.

Once I tapped into that feeling—filled with excitement and an overwhelming sense of accomplishment—I signed the card. To commemorate the moment, I took a photo of the signed replica and shared it with Rudy, my competition buddy Patricia, and our competition prep coach, Kim Oddo of *Oddo's Angels*. These three were my accountability partners. Then finally, I pinned the dream card to my vision board.

I originally planned to end the season with *NPC's Team Universe* Competition in Teaneck, New Jersey that July. It was one of the East Coast's highly anticipated national amateur competitions. For women, there were four categories in which to compete:

- **Women's Bodybuilding**: Often likened to the "She-Hulks" of the world, showcasing extreme muscle mass and definition.
- **Bikini**: The lean, toned, and ultra-feminine extreme opposite of bodybuilding—think "Bikini Barbie."
- **Physique**: Positioned between bodybuilding and figure, this category emphasizes muscle tone and symmetry while maintaining a softer aesthetic than bodybuilding.
- **Figure**: The softer of the two middle categories, offering a balance of shape, tone, and elegance, with a focus on overall symmetry.

I was a solid figure competitor—too much lean muscle for bikini and not quite enough for physique. The four female divisions were further broken down into sub-groups based on height. Those groups were known as *classes*.

I was excited to place first in my class, competing against over 15 figure athletes. But unexpectedly, I didn't win the coveted pro card that night. Instead of awarding the card to the winners of each class (as had been done in the past), the judges compared the winners of the six figure classes and gave pro cards to only the top two overall winners.

"Oh well" I thought. "I guess I'll have to try again next year." With that, I was done for the season. Kim tried to convince me to compete in the *IFBB North American* competition in Pittsburgh in two weeks, but I already had plans to take the boys to my mother-in-law's vacation home down the Jersey Shore. The house was about 12 minutes from Long Beach Island, and I was ready for some much-needed downtime.

My girlfriend Victoria (Vicki for short) was joining us with her two sons, Nick, and David, who are slightly older than Rudy and Sean. Big Rudy had another week of work before his vacation began and Tiera (age 23) was off doing her own thing. Rudy and Sean were already on break, and it was the perfect time to reconnect with my girl while letting the boys enjoy some fun in the sun.

Aside from having the week pre-planned, I could already taste the sweet, tart flavor of the creamy key lime pie from Ahern's Fish Market. It has always been one of my summer favorites. As far as competing again that year was concerned, I was mentally and physically exhausted. I needed to recharge… and eat key lime pie.

Leave it to a true friend to put things into perspective. Vicki arrived with the boys, a few swimsuit options, a nice bottle of wine for her and Patron silver for me. A little tequila pairs perfectly with key lime pie. While the crew settled in, I shared with Vicki, "So Kim wants me to compete again in two weeks." Vicki turned to me and gave me a side eye look. "As much as I would love to hang and crush this fabulous bottle with you", raising the bottle of tequila as she spoke. "I'm thinking you should do it, Kenny." (Vicki calls me Kenny for short.)

I tried giving Vicki all the excuses in the world as to why I shouldn't do it—the registration deadline already passed, not to mention, I'd already eaten more than half of that pie, which would not have been on my diet regimen if I were planning to compete. "If you don't do it, you may regret it, but you won't regret it if you do it." Vicki's words rang true.

I decided to contact the show's promoter to see if they would make an exception, considering I just placed first in the most recent East Coast National competition. Not long after sending the email, I received a response instructing me to mail in the application and the fee as soon as possible.

"Are you going to go get your pro card or are they going to have to mail it to you?" she teased.

Vicki has always been a great motivator and a source of inspiration for me. In fact, when I was 23, Vicki was the one who encouraged me to go back to school.

At that time, we were working together at Lace, a bikini bar in Wayne, New Jersey. "Kenny, they will literally pay for you to go to school!" She emphasized, excitedly explaining Federal Student Aid. She even brought me a FAFSA (Free Application for Federal Student Aid) form, which afforded me the ability to attend NYSID.

After applying for school and completing the FAFSA, I was surprised and elated to learn that I qualified not only for financial aid, but I also received a small scholarship from one of the school's funds and was given the opportunity to work in the school's resource library. *(Sidenote: If you haven't donated to your alma mater's scholarship fund, consider it—you could contribute to the development of a student like me. How cool would that be?)*

After completing the competition application, I booked my flight to Pittsburgh. Heartbroken, I threw out the last bit of key lime pie (if I couldn't eat it, no one could). We then ventured to the Vitamin Shoppe to stock up on protein powder, branch chain amino acid (BCAA), and a pre-workout supplement before stopping into a sporting goods store to grab a jump rope.

I hadn't brought any workout gear to the shore with me since I was focused on being off-season, but with a quick mental reset, I jumped back into prep mode. I started doing bodyweight workouts and cardio at the house, squeezing in training between trips to the beach and Fantasy Island, an amusement park nearby the kids liked.

Fast-forward to competition weekend. I traveled solo, as summer vacation was over. The boys returned to school and Rudy was back at work. My mind and body—I was as ready as I was going to be. It was then that I decided no matter what happened, this would be my last NPC competition.

I felt guilty about having had the key lime pie a few weeks prior, wondering if anyone could *see* it. At that point, though, it was going to be whatever it was. I was there and *my package*, complete with bronzer and oil, was the best I could present at that time. No matter what happened, *not going for it* wouldn't be a regret I owned.

I looked at myself in the mirror to make sure everything was tucked in properly and took a few minutes to practice my posing. I wore a stunning metallic blue bikini given to me by IFBB Figure Pro, Teresa Anthony. It was adorned in red and clear rhinestones, giving it an overall patriotic feel. I finished the look with a pair of see-through slingback stiletto Pleasers and my hair styled in loose, flowing curls.

Talk about manifesting! Let's pause and talk about the first time I met Teresa Anthony. Being one of the most beautiful African-American women I'd ever seen grace the IFBB Pro Figure stage, Teresa was one of my all-time favorite figure competitors. I remember watching footage of her online from competitions past. I even used an image of her on my vision board for motivation. (Yep, the same board that held the pro card I created to help manifest the pro win.) When it came to figure, Teresa Anthony and Meriza DeGuzman were it for me. Through their energy and accomplishments, I could see possibility.

Earlier that year, while washing my hands in the restroom at *Arnold Schwarzenegger's Sports Festival* in Columbus, Ohio, I looked up and, in the mirror, I saw her! At first, I thought I must be mistaken, but it was really Teresa Anthony! Of course, I had to tell her I was a huge fan. How could I not? I couldn't have been more excited.

The encounter with Teresa made my whole trip. We exchanged contact information and connected via phone shortly after the festival. Teresa shared some training and posing tips. She even gifted me the beautiful blue suit I wore in Pittsburgh.

During bodybuilding competitions, each contestant walks across the stage as their name and contestant number are announced. "Number 674, Kenyatta Jones-Arietta." I put on a happy face and strutted to center stage, wearing the Teresa Anthony gifted stunner. I executed my turns and poses before exiting stage right.

After all the competitors in my class did their walks, the top five were called back to pose together. "Number 674." I made it to the top five. As I stood on stage, holding my pose and my smile, I also held on to the thought, *this is the last time I am doing an NPC show*. "Quarter turn," the head judge called out. We five pivoted as one, flexing our muscles, giving the judges every opportunity to examine the definition of our lean, chiseled physiques.

"Quarter turn," the head judge repeated. Again, we all turned. And again, I repeated to myself, *this is the last NPC show I'm doing*. The five of us smiled and waved at the audience as we exited the stage. One of the other finalists in the Figure E category seemed to be the local favorite for some of the other competitors in our class. As we all walked off stage and headed back to the dressing room, I overheard a few of their comments.

"Oh my God, girl, you crushed it!" "You got this! You look amazing!" At that moment, I honestly didn't care anymore. All I knew was this was my last NPC show. Competition prep was grueling, and if I didn't win the pro card this time, I was ready to accept it just may not have been in the cards for me.

The meal preps, the workouts, the check-ins—on top of raising the kids and work—it was a lot. In the dressing room, I lay flat on my back, in a black satin robe on the carpeted floor, legs elevated against the wall. I called Rudy to fill him in on how the morning went. Boy, was I starting to regret throwing out that key lime pie.

The winners of the competitions aren't announced until the evening show, with the grand finale being the crowning of the men's bodybuilding competition champion—the buff, super-sized cherry on top. The time in between the morning and evening sessions was spent resting and taking in some carbs to make muscles pop for the evening presentation. Somewhere in there, I may have managed a cat nap.

I snacked on a few slices of baked sweet potato. They were cut like thick potato chips, but soft, with only cinnamon and a little sea salt sprinkled on top. I ate them with a side of cold, bland tilapia, and washed it down with a few sips of water—just enough to stay hydrated without risking bloating and ruining my look for the night.

When the evening program reached figure class E category, all competitors walked across the stage and formed two lines upstage. We stood there, all smiles, as the announcer called the top five finalists to center stage. My name was called—I officially made it to the finals.

The finalists lined up, and one by one, each competitor was announced, stepping forward as placements were revealed from fifth to first place. When it came time to announce the first-place finalist, my name was called out as the winner! It took a moment to process, but the reaction from the competitors standing next to me made it clear—I won!

Talk about being on cloud nine. All of the hard work (and the tossing of the key lime) paid off. Just like that, my affirmation and vision board dreams both came true. As I'd declared, that was *the last* NPC show I ever did. 2012, the year I wrote on the makeshift pro card pinned to my vision board, became the year my dream of becoming a professional figure competitor turned into reality.

I visualized it, I created and lived the feeling of winning, and I put in the work. Remember, it's not just thinking about it—action must be taken. And to think, I'd almost given up on my goal of achieving the pro card that year. Sometimes we don't realize how close we are to accomplishing our dreams when we are ready to throw in the towel.

If you are being led to give your unrealized goal one more shot, go for it! You have nothing to lose but a little more time, and everything to gain. You just don't know how close you may be.

※

Many people give up on their dreams not realizing how close they are to achieving them. Persistence can be the key to actualizing the love and life you desire.

Don't get it twisted, though—I'm not suggesting you stay in that dead-end relationship with the narcissist you've been *on-again, off again* with for the past five years. But I *am* saying, don't give up on the possibility of a strong, loving connection with someone just because the last one didn't work out.

It's not merely enough to want to be in love. It has to be the right kind of love in order to sustain. Sometimes, the only way to truly understand what we really want in love and life is by experiencing what we don't want. This brings me back to John Assaraf's words about *manifesting correctly*.

It's important to understand that sometimes we manifest the wrong way, which can lead us to the opposite of what we desire. For instance, if you've witnessed or experienced a relationship where someone was verbally or physically abusive, it's essential to be mindful of how you frame your intentions when manifesting what it is you want.

Instead of saying, "I don't want to be in a physically or verbally abusive relationship," avoid using words like *"abusive, toxic or dysfunctional,"* as focusing on those terms can unintentionally attract more of those behaviors. It's extremely important to focus on the positive; What you DO want, as opposed to acknowledging what you DON'T want.

Use phrases such as, "I am in a beautiful relationship with someone who loves, respects and adores me... and gives me the most amazing massages." (You can thank me for that one later). Or perhaps, "I am in a loving relationship with someone who offers only kind words of encouragement." Manifest positive outcomes by focusing solely on what you want to attract, not what you want to avoid.

I often share with people—depending on their religious beliefs—that the Bible suggests God gave us the power that *He Himself* possesses: the power to create through words. Consider Genesis 1:1-3 in the Old Testament. Read it and tell me—How did God create heaven and earth?

It is not often that people answer this correctly right away, even after just reading the words.

Taken from the King James Version of the Bible:

1. In the beginning God created the heaven and the earth.
2. And the earth was without form, and void; and darkness was upon the face of the deep. And the Spirit of God moved upon the face of the waters.
3. And God said, Let there be light: and there was light.

And right there is the answer. *He* said it. God spoke words to create. Words hold significant power.

No, I am not religious, though raised in a very Christian household. And I do mean raised. My grandparents were a deacon and deaconess of Greater St. James Fire Baptized Holiness Church of God and the Americas, located in the Woodbridge section of Detroit. Between Sunday School, Bible study, choir rehearsal, building board meetings, and Wednesday and Friday night services, my cousin Renee, and I were literally in church four to six days a week. No joke! I tease that I did enough time in church before age seventeen to last the rest of my days.

Although I don't participate in organized religion today, I do know, with all that I am, that there is something greater within and around all of us. Whether you believe in God, Jehovah, Allah, Buddha, or nothing at all, know that you can find valuable life nuggets in almost every religious scripture, including the pages of the Holy Bible. I can't recall exactly when those first three verses of the Old Testament began to resonate with me, though I do know it was sometime in the past eleven years. Understanding the power of words is one thing that has made the most sense to me in this life.

Words. Create. Reality.

A few years ago, I attended a dinner party with some of my single girlfriends. The words they used were fascinating—and revealed why they might still be single. "There are no good men left out there," one of them said. Another added, "All the good men are either married or don't have jobs," and, "These guys today are full of it!"

It wasn't the right time or place to challenge them. I was clearly the odd woman out, but what they didn't realize was that by making those statements with the power of belief behind them, they were turning their declarations into their reality. It's simply that easy to do.

If you find yourself voicing similar statements, I challenge you to change your words and your mindset. It is impossible to see any good men or women out there if you are constantly affirming that there are none. Change your words, and you will change your world. Remember, you can't manifest positive things using negative words.

This practice doesn't only apply to love—it's also relevant to finances, health, your profession, and all other aspects of your life. The power to create the reality we want lies within each of us, and its forceful energy resides in our words, our emotions, and our actions.

RECOGNIZING LOVE

*"I walk down the same street. There is a deep
hole in the sidewalk. I fall in."*

—Portia Nelson,
There's a Hole in My Sidewalk.

I remember the first time one of my exes shared those lines with me. Years later, like deja vu, another did the same. Each was trying to show me the patterns I couldn't yet see for myself. I started to wonder if all my love interests had read the same book.

Recognizing love is not always as easy as one would think—especially if, like me, you've historically had a *different* idea of what your love would be like… remember, I dated the *same* guy again, and again… and again. Some habits linger until you consciously decide to break the cycle.

I only dated one real monster. For the most part, the men I dated were interesting human beings and super talented. One of my *ghosts of boyfriends past* was the proprietor of a popular and trendy restaurant in New York City. Another was a creative director for a Fortune 500 company. I briefly dated a musician and an industrial product designer. No, not at the same time, but hey! Who's judging?

I went out with quite a few entrepreneurs. (Actually, most of my suitors harbored entrepreneurial spirit animals.) I dated a police officer, a drug dealer, a doctor, a stockbroker; a photographer, a trust fund baby, God's gift to women, and most famously, an up-and-coming actor who later turned out to be a very popular action movie star. Who would've thunk it? But no, I don't kiss and tell.

Through each of those relationships, I learned a lot about food, fashion, art, music, design, drugs, night clubs, sexuality, personalities (multiple), hospitality, party promoting, and the list goes on. But with each connection, when the relationship reached a point where it was time to move forward or move on... We just stopped moving.

This I finally recognized as a pattern. I was attracted to men who were fun to experience any and everything with, with the exception of a committed relationship with plans of a future together. Yep, that part. Looking back over my dating history, I can't help but wonder if I unconsciously chose the same type of partner to ensure things *wouldn't* go further. While I felt the sting that inevitably comes with breakups, the excitement was always in the promise of new love.

Similar to Gillian Owens in *Practical Magic*. Gillian went for fleeting, often impulsive connections—until one romantic suitor, Jimmy, became dangerously obsessed. Working in strip clubs, I encountered a few obsessive characters I had to be mindful of. I can recall instances where patrons would try to follow me home or when an ex I had broken up with just happened to show up alone at the same restaurant I brunched at. It was obvious he wasn't there to dine with anyone else. I found it to be a little creepy, but ultimately harmless.

As I shared previously, I did have one really awful experience during my dating years. And what I can tell you from that experience is this, when someone shows you *who* they are and what they are capable of, believe them. Glossing over an abusive incident I witnessed between an ex and his cousin landed me in a midtown Manhattan precinct, filing a police report against him several months later. It's like the old adage, *"Fool me once, shame on you."* I vowed never to let anything like that happen to me again.

I wrestled with whether or not to share the details of the actual event because of its intensity, but in the end, I decided it may be helpful just in case you find yourself in a similar situation. And if you recognize that you are seeing some of the same signs, consider this your wake-up call, my friend.

I was around 20 at the time. My then boyfriend, let's call him *Don*, brought me out to Brooklyn to visit his mom, Helen. Helen was one of the sweetest humans I've ever met, and she was extremely helpful with Tiera, who was around three when Don and I dated. You could think of Helen as Tiera's *unofficial* grandmother... or fairy godmother even. She lived in a townhouse in the East New York section of Brooklyn, next door to her sister, Doris.

While at the house, Don encountered his cousin, Tanya, who lived in the lower-level apartment of the early 1900's brownstone. I don't know what the two were arguing about. The cause of the altercation is irrelevant, but it escalated to Don pinning Tanya up against the wall with his right hand gripped firmly around her neck. Tanya's feet barely touched the floor as she fought in an attempt to get away. She struggled to maintain her balance and like a fish out of water, her eyes began to bulge as her breath was restricted by Don's clutch. I was stunned!

I'd never seen that side of Don before. I had absolutely no idea it even existed. He was always so happy, walking around with this killer smile and calm demeanor. But that day—I still get chills recounting the event. It was like witnessing "Dr. Jekell and Mr. Hyde" come to life. Don went from being a pleasant, happy-go-lucky gentleman to this outlandish, unrecognizable thug that I would normally have had nothing to do with.

Thank God his mother was there. Helen, the peacemaker, managed to convince Don to let Tanya go—quite literally to release the hold he had on her neck. He finally relented. Thankfully, Tanya wasn't seriously injured aside from the blood vessel that popped in her eye. While I felt a wave of relief, I was still in shock. After the incident, Don seamlessly slipped back into his kind and charming self. The monster returned to a man as if nothing out of the ordinary had ever happened.

I was so naïve, I thought what I saw—what he did—couldn't possibly be who he was. It just couldn't be. But shortly after, during a visit to my mom in Detroit, Don and I got into an argument while running errands. I don't remember where we were coming from, but I do remember being so pissed at him that, when the car idled at a traffic light, I jumped out. Without looking back, I started walking down the boulevard to cool off.

Don pulled over, jumped out of the car, and pursued me. He grabbed me by the neck and before I could process what was happening, I found myself on the ground. I lay there, on the grass, in broad daylight, with his hands around my throat. "Don't ever leave me like that again!" he demanded.

I looked up at him, the sun shining brightly from behind his silhouette, illuminating the moment. *Oh my God! He's going to kill me!*, I thought. He released me before long. We regrouped and returned to the car in silence.

Believe it or not, I thought I must have done something to deserve his punishment. While at the same time thinking, *how could he do this to me and say he loves me? Did he love me too much? This couldn't be normal and it definitely wasn't acceptable behavior.*

You would think that would've been enough for me to tell Don to take a hike and never look back… but no, it wasn't. He had been so good to me up to that point, I didn't know which version of him was really him. There was no way this aggressive lunatic could be my Don—the man I knew and loved—could it? I honestly didn't know what to think.

Shortly after our return to New York, Don and I got into another fight. This time we were in my apartment, and this time it escalated. Most of the details are a blur, but what I do remember was horrifying. I don't recall how he got my clothes off or even what I was wearing. But I do remember being choked to the point of exhaustion before being sodomized. *What part of him thought this was okay? How could he take pleasure in hurting me this way?*

I begged him to stop. He ignored my plea. I was terrified he was really going to kill me this time. It was so hard to believe what was happening. *Is this how my life ends?*, I wondered. Then something in me snapped—I went into survival mode. I shifted from fighting to convincing him I liked it, hoping desperately to calm his energy and regain my strength. Slowly, he began to ease his grip, though he hadn't stopped violating me.

"*I need water,*" I croaked, my voice raspy and broken like a dying frog. My throat parched from the screaming and the pressure from his hands making it worse. He stepped into the kitchen, wearing nothing from the waist down. That was my opportunity. Without hesitation, I bolted!

Completely naked, I ran out of my apartment and sprinted upstairs to a neighbor's flat. I will forever be grateful she was home—and that she let me in. Breathlessly, I told her about the attack. We walked to her bathroom where she draped her bathrobe around my shoulders and grabbed her landline to call the police.

While we anxiously awaited their arrival, we could hear Don knocking on the doors of the neighboring apartments, searching for me. When he reached her door, I hid in the bathroom, my heart pounding like a beating drum.

"Hi. How can I help you?" She answered the door calmly.

"It's Don—I'm looking for Kenyatta. Have you seen her?"

"No. Is everything ok?" she asked, trying to act normal.

"No. All good. Thanks." He moved on and continued his search.

Hey neighbor—you know who you are. I can't thank you enough for being there for me. You may have saved my life that night and you are forever my hero.

There was another knock at the door. "Who is it?" she asked.

This time it was the police. She opened the door to let them in. They spoke with me briefly before escorting me back to my apartment to get dressed. Don was already in their custody and had been taken to the station. Like a celebrity being whisked away from the paparazzi, I was transported to the precinct in a second car to file a formal complaint.

Don—my boyfriend, my assailant.

At the station, I identified him in a line up. A group of men was presented to me like bodybuilders on a stage being called out to pose for judging.

"Turn to your right," an officer commanded.

I thought this stuff only happened in movies.

I grunted to clear my swollen throat. *"That's him,"* I rasped when Don turned to face me through the one-way glass. Like Clark Kent, he stood wearing prescription glasses and a deceiving mask of innocence.

"That's him." His buttoned-down white-collar shirt and khaki Dockers were severely wrinkled from his night in the cell. Don was an imposter. He was an abuser. He was no Clark Kent, and he definitely was no Superman— but I couldn't follow through with pressing charges.

One of the officers tried persuading me to move forward with the complaint. He looked me in the eyes, his expression filled with disappointment, but all I could think of was Don's mother, Helen. She came to pick me up from the station that night. She asked me not to press charges. Out of my love for her and the bond we shared, I granted her wish.

Don and I broke up for good after that incident. I didn't need to learn any other lesson of that kind. Looking back, I realize I probably should have moved forward with pursuing legal action. Don assaulted me. He assaulted his cousin. We can't be the only two. Tanya probably wasn't the first, and unfortunately, I doubt I was the last. Maya Angelou once said, "When someone shows you who they are, believe them." If only I had.

I give myself grace for not having the courage to press charges against him back then. It was **Survival 101**—though part of me ached to stand up for myself, at that point in my journey, I was still alone in a vast, fast-paced city. Helen was the only person I knew I could truly depend on. Tears filled her eyes when she pleaded with me not to press charges against her son. I couldn't bear the thought of hurting her or jeopardizing our relationship and her support—even if she had raised a closeted beast.

I came to recognize that what Don and I had wasn't love… and I would subject myself to his rage no longer. Looking back, there were other signs that he may not have been right for me that I ignored. Intimately, sometimes I felt *dirty* after we were together—just like something wasn't right. What I experienced with Don made me much more cautious moving forward. I began paying closer attention to the little things, but I wouldn't give up on the idea of someday connecting with a loving partner who would never hurt me.

∽

Years later, when Rudy presented himself to me, our relationship was very different from anything I had experienced before. So much so I didn't initially recognize that he fit the description of the partner I'd asked the Universe to bring into my life less than a year earlier. It would have been awesome if the Cosmos just put a bow around his neck, sat him in front of my door, and rang and ran—but where would the fun be in that?

With the connection we had you'd think I would have recognized who he was right away. We could almost read each other's minds, often predicting what the other would say before the words even left our lips. We even had a little trick we'd do. One of us would write down what the other was going to say, then reveal it after the words had been spoken. We'd wake up talking to each other. I mean literally talking in our sleep, only to wake up in the middle of a full-on conversation. *Who does that?*

Twenty-six years later, Rudy and I are still deeply connected—in some ways, even more so. How was it remotely possible that I didn't immediately realize he was "*the one*" back then? After many years of reflecting on our unshakable bond, I now understand that my inability to *see* my iron love for who he was comes down to a single, one syllable word that tends to get in the way of many people realizing their dreams: FEAR.

If, when I suggested that a one-syllable word is the culprit, your first thought wasn't "fear," but "YOU," you are 100% correct. It is *you* who allows fear to creep in, convincing you to walk away from your ultimate dreams and desires.

Before I was forced to face my fear head-on, I almost allowed my doubts to scheme me out of some of the most amazing moments of my life. The journey toward overcoming fear and insecurity has taught me that love isn't just a feeling—it's a choice we make, again and again, even in the face of uncertainty.

OVERCOMING FEAR

"He's too short."
"She has a child with someone else."
"He's not a good dresser."
"She has ugly feet."

When you look at the big picture of life, those reservations really don't matter. What does matter is:

"He is great with my children."
"We always have the best time together."
"I can be my complete self with her."
"We have the most amazing connection."
"We fill each other's cups."

Over the years, I've watched as others (friends, family, employees and clients) let fear stop them in their pursuit of love, enterprise, personal growth, and even their most deeply held dreams. As a spectator, it's easier to see the overall situation when you're not part of the equation. Sometimes, the ideal choice appears to be glaringly obvious to those not emotionally invested.

When attempting to make sound decisions, if you are coming from a place of fear, you may overlook critical details or over analyze them to the point of talking yourself out of a potentially great opportunity. Fear ushers in doubts that cripple, making the leap toward fulfillment feel impossible.

After nearly twelve months working on my writing project, I began the search for a literary agent. I connected with a rep who suggested I reach out to a few publicists to help grow my online presence to increase my chances of securing a traditional publishing deal. One renowned publicist showed interest in my story but offered a caveat. *"You're not a doctor. I couldn't put you on a stage with relationship specialists,"* she advised. *"But success—you're the poster child for success."*

For months, I grappled with the idea of changing the context of my work. I didn't love the idea, but in an effort to make the manuscript more appealing to a publisher, I seriously considered her suggestion. Yet *Iron Success* just wasn't resonating with me. I didn't feel it, and trying to force it would have been a betrayal of my own truth.

Then came the fear—fear of making the *wrong decision* paralyzed me for almost a year. Don't get me wrong, I stayed busy with other projects, I just stopped writing. Around the same time, I was accepted into and decided to participate in the *Goldman Sachs 10,000 Small Businesses program*—a rigorous, accelerated 14-week business masterclass. Meanwhile, *Iron Love* remained untouched, suspended in the cloud, waiting for its moment to shine.

As I often say, the Universe sends us *signs* to help guide us. Shortly after graduating from 10kSB, I planned a girls' weekend at our cabin in Northern Michigan. After four months of intense focus on my real estate business, I was ready for a break. A few of my childhood friends were driving up from Southern Michigan, while I was flying in from New York to Detroit, with a connecting flight to Traverse City. The plan was for me to stay overnight at a hotel near Cherry Capital Airport, pick up a rental car the next morning, and drive up to meet them at RiverHouse Cabin. The cabin is about an hour and forty minutes from Traverse City—just far enough to feel like a true escape.

As Rudy and I loaded my bags into the car en route to JFK, my phone started pinging with text notifications. My flight from New York was delayed due to inclement weather. I could feel stress lurking around my neck, tightening around my shoulders and upper back. The connecting flight to Traverse City was the last one out that evening—making it in time would require nothing short of a miracle. To calm myself, I started repeating the following affirmations:

There is a reason I'm not supposed to make that flight.
The delay is for my benefit.

Everything is in divine order.

Let me tell you, when you make a conscious decision to stay positive in the face of disruption, it becomes easier to navigate the situation and uncover the *why*. There is always a deeper-seated reason behind the perceived misfortune, even if it's not easy to see in the moment.

Sometimes, when we're caught in the heat of it, emotionally off balance or not in the right headspace, we can miss the greater lesson. When I realized there was no way I was going to make the connecting flight, it took extreme effort to stay positive, but I managed. And I pivoted. Before I landed, Rudy canceled my reservation at the Hampton Inn in Traverse City and booked me a room at the Omni Hotel in Detroit Metropolitan Airport.

Once off the plane, I went straight to baggage claim, retrieved my luggage, and headed directly to the Omni. Upon receiving my room key, I made my way over to the hotel bar for a bourbon and a burger. After soothing the raging beast also known as my belly, I lifted my gaze from my empty plate and took in the scene. To my right sat a man I recognized from the lobby—he checked in just before I did and disappeared toward the elevators. He must have dropped off his bags and returned to the bar.

We introduced ourselves and quickly fell into easy conversation. His name was Antonio, and within minutes, we realized we had quite a bit in common, including the fact that he has a sister named Kenyetta (off by one letter). Even more interesting, neither of us was supposed to be there—he, too, had missed a flight heading out west and was unexpectedly stranded in Detroit for the evening. We shared stories about moving out of Michigan, having both left *The Mitten State* many years prior. We talked about real estate, travel, and family. Towards the end of our conversation, I asked what he did for a living.

"I'm an author and motivational speaker," he replied—the very thing I see myself doing in this next phase of my life.

Wow! I thought. *This was not a coincidence.*

I shared that I had spent most of 2023 working on the manuscript for my first book. Antonio's response was immediate, "From what you've shared, sis, you have to get your story out there. I actually have someone I want to connect you with."

We exchanged contact info, paid our bills, and called it a night. It had been a very long, yet unexpectedly profound, day. It soon became even more apparent that we were meant to meet that evening. We left the restaurant and ended up in the same elevator. We got off on the same floor. We walked down the same corridor. Our rooms were literally right next to each other.

"601", I commented, instinctively adding the digits together, as I often do. "That's a seven".

Antonio smiled, "Seven is actually my lucky number."

How funny, I thought. But the synchronicity didn't stop there—seven also happened to be Antonio's last name spelled backward.

The next morning, we didn't see each other, though I sent a quick text to say it was a pleasure meeting. As I left the hotel, I was still on cloud nine, reflecting on our chance encounter. But my journey was just beginning. There were no available flights to Traverse City that morning. At that point, it made more sense to rent a car and road trip it up to the cabin, an easy four-hour tour. I called an Uber and headed to Enterprise Car Rental, a short distance from the airport.

As I walked inside, I couldn't help but notice a woman standing to my right. She wore a white basketball jersey with bold blue letters across the back that read: Big Booty 7.

I had to snap a photo.

"*Looks like your number is following me*", I texted Antonio.

From that day forward, the number seven has been popping up everywhere. Seven months from that night, I finally recognized that it was a sign—my sign—to get back to writing. Due in part to that seemingly random encounter that felt fated, you are now holding and flipping the pages of (or listening to) the very project I told Antonio about.

᧥

When we operate in fear mode, we can become so afraid of making the *wrong* decision that we end up making choices that don't align with what we say we want. I hesitate to label these decisions "mistakes" because, in truth, they are lessons—lessons that still need to be learned. Lessons are not mistakes, even if they come with a few bumps or take more than a few tries to grasp. Learning from our "mistakes" or life lessons is what growing and experiencing life are all about.

This fear-based pattern doesn't limit itself to love. As we saw in my writing journey, it can present itself in every aspect of life—business ventures, career decisions, parenting, you name it.

Even in real estate, I've had countless conversations with aspiring first-time investors eager to jump into the rental market. Time and again, I've listened to stories of how *fear* and doubt kept them stuck in their own heads, ultimately talking themselves out of taking the leap.

"What if I can't rent it?"

"What if I end up with a horrible tenant and can't get them out?"

By the time they're finally ready to jump in, the opportunity has passed.

Speaking of jumping in, I am proud to share, I recently took a *leap of faith*— from the top of a waterfall. I may seem fearless to you but let me be crystal clear—I was terrified!

I've had plenty of opportunities to go cliff jumping during past vacations, but I could never talk myself into *actually* doing it.

Oddly enough, a few years ago, I had no problem talking myself into jumping out of a perfectly good airplane while riding tandem with a cameraman *in my face*—from approximately 13,500 feet in the air. And had the audacity to pose for a picture while free-falling at 120 miles per hour. Yet a thirteen-foot drop into a natural wonder had me shook.

My rationalization for skydiving? I'd known about *Skydive the Ranch* for over 20 years. If it wasn't safe, it would've been shut down by now. Plus, the tandem instructor I was jumping with was only 21—his life was just beginning. There was no way he wanted to die that day.

But cliff jumping? That's a different story.

Rudy and I were on vacation with our friends Alex and Alexandra in the Dominican Republic. We were visiting the Damajagua Waterfalls when I finally decided it was time to finally face my fear. I wanted so badly to jump this time.

I stood on earth's edge, watching as people—young, old, big, and small—all took the leap, wearing life vests, helmets, water shoes and carefree smiles. They splashed into the basin below and quickly popped back up to the water's surface, bobbling like buoys. Meanwhile, I stood frozen, my feet practically cemented to the ground. It was frustrating—actually infuriating—to feel so paralyzed while everyone else made it look so effortless.

Rudy took the leap before I did. Watching him work through his own fear gave me the courage to work through mine. He took a deep breath; you could see his chest rise and fall, as if a doctor armed with a stethoscope was checking his lungs.

Rudy adjusted his chin strap, tapping his helmet like he was playing "Head, Shoulders, Knees, and Toes." He took two steps toward the left railing, resting his hand on top, moving closer to the edge, peering down to analyze the pool's depth. Then, with a shift of his hips, he centered himself on the boardwalk. I felt like I was watching a new dance—The *Rudy Rumba*.

He walked back over to the left side, resting his hip on the side rail. With his arms at his sides, he stepped back to the center and glanced over at us, almost as if he were looking to see if we were still there. Rudy gave the right railing a quick tap before returning to center, taking the right foot forward, tapping twice, and then—he jumped.

THAT was a process.

Now, I know that reads like a lot of time passed with all the steps but based on the video recording of the actual event, Rudy's plank pacing was only about 14 seconds. Most people let fear stop them for much longer than that.

Experiencing Rudy's transition from fear to determination, combined with the momentum from the others who jumped before me, gave me the courage to go for it. I decided on a smaller jump first though—and even that took some negotiating. Once I took the plunge, a surge of confidence (and adrenaline) rushed through me, leaving me pumped and ready for the next adventure.

The fear we create in our minds is so much greater than the thing we actually fear. There is a well-known Mark Twain quote in which the acclaimed writer says, "I've had a lot of worries in my life, most of which never happened." Fear and worry take up much more head space then they deserve. With my newfound clarity, I returned to the higher cliff—and this time, I jumped.

I have only the fear of losing Rudy to thank for my decision to finally work through my doubt of being in a real relationship with him. I enjoyed what we had, but I thought he deserved someone who could go the distance. How could I possibly be that person? I wasn't convinced that I was.

I was (and still am) older, with more *worldly* experiences. I was already a mom, from a totally different community, and I was a stripper to boot. Which leads me to question: I manifested Rudy—but did some part of me believe I wasn't *deserving* of the kind of love I longed for? He loved me so deeply, and it showed.

Now, as I've grown, I see that love for what it truly is. I *am* deserving of his love, and fully accept and appreciate his devotion.

You, too, are deserving of real love. We all are. But are you willing to confront your fear of unworthiness, fear of rejection, fear of heartbreak and/or fear of making a mistake to do the work to make it your reality? Are you ready to commit? Or are you just somewhat interested?

My journey to love and self-discovery taught me that accepting love, especially from ourselves, is often the hardest part. It's as if we're conditioned to feel undeserving of the happiness we desire. Shakti Gawain captures this sentiment perfectly in her book, *Creative Visualization*:

"In order to use creative visualization to create what you want in life; you must be willing and able to accept the best that life has to offer you."

"Strange as it may seem, many of us have difficulty accepting the possibility of having what we want in life. This usually stems from some feeling of unworthiness, which we took on at a very early age."

Recognizing our worth is one thing, but sometimes, it takes a wake-up call to realize that what we desire won't wait around forever.

The night I finally realized that what I wanted could slip through my fingers, Rudy arrived early to pick me up from work. He was eager to share some exciting news.

He reached into his pocket and pulled out a little folded piece of paper, which he opened to reveal a woman's name and number. "I'm going to go out with her," he shared with a smile, awaiting the reaction you would expect from a *friend* who has been giving you advice that you finally decide to take. I remember thinking, "Oh shit! I fucked up." And with that realization, our path began to change.

I'm sure he could tell by the dumbfounded look on my face that I wasn't thrilled with the idea—but wasn't it what I wanted? I'd been pushing him away and trying to get him to go out with other people, but I was taken aback when he actually put plans in motion.

I tried playing it off as though I was okay with it. I may have sorely forgotten to flash a fake smile. I wanted to be happy for him, but what about us? As my shift was ending, I told Rudy not to worry about giving me a ride home that night; I would find my own way—a way to start distancing myself from him.

"Don't be silly!" He insisted. "I'll give you a ride."

After changing into my street clothes and grabbing my bag of tricks (costumes, heels, make-up and toiletries), I plopped into his car, and we drove away in silence. It was the looooooongest 45 minutes... EVER!

When we got to Jamaica (Queens that is), Rudy got off the Van Wyck at Exit 4. We were immediately greeted by a red light. That's when I was struck by the thought:

"Life is like a road," I started.

"You come to a red light; you stop. You can decide whether to continue on that road, or you can choose to take a left, keep straight, or even turn around and go back in the opposite direction." I analyzed the moment.

Aside from literally being stopped at a red light, Rudy's decision to start dating felt like a definite *red light* in our relationship.

"I don't want to date anyone else, but you keep pushing me away. So, I'm doing what you said you want me to do," Rudy confessed.

He was beginning to accept that maybe it really was just a case of "right person, wrong time" for us.

Hearing his confession was my *aha* moment. The next decision would alter the course of our lives forever: should we continue on the path that could lead to *"us,"* or would it be best to go our separate ways?

Well, being that I've written a book about our love, you already know the answer. The light turned green, and with our seatbelts fastened, we turned the radio up and drove full steam ahead into the direction of our future together.

As you may have suspected, Rudy didn't end up calling to set up a date with that woman—we moved forward, and he never looked back.

I am grateful for her presence, though. Their brief encounter was my wake-up call and the catalyst for Rudy's and my decision to move forward. (*Sorry but thank you.*)

※

But that's just my story—you don't *need* the presence of another person to recognize love for what it is. If you're questioning the love relationship you're in and looking for clarity as to whether it's the right one for you, you need only *search your soul* for answers. If you're willing to be honest with yourself, YOU will be the best barometer.

Sit somewhere alone, in silence and focus on your connection with your love and the time you spend together.

How does that connection make you feel?

If it drains you, makes you feel weak, or leaves you feeling lesser—like you're not enough or as though something is wrong with you—it may not be the right situation for you.

If you feel loved, supported, and empowered, continue on the road to see where it leads. If the effects of the relationship are positive, what do you have to lose? But if you've noticed any major red flags that you're ignoring or making excuses for, DON'T! Remember my situation with Don. Rose-colored glasses could cost you more than you're willing to pay.

Reminiscing about that momentous car ride with Rudy back to my place—I had a whole lifetime of love, happiness, kids, grandkids, a dog, and many adventures to lose had I let fear rule. You too have a life of love and happiness waiting for you. But you'll only realize it on the other side of fear.

When your manifestation of love has come to fruition, the likelihood of it scaring you is great. Your heart palpitates, and you question yourself:

"Am I making a mistake?"

"How do I know that this is truly the right person for me?"

Questioning is human nature, but the instinct to question things doesn't mean you're making the wrong decision. We, as humans, tend to resist the things that are unfamiliar. That hazy confusion that comes just before clarity—it's like the storm before the still. A natural moment of hesitation, maybe even a built-in safety mechanism or maybe just prior conditioning, keeping us from rushing into truth too fast.

When you're learning something new—whether it's a math equation, how to play a musical instrument, how to speak a new language, or any other new skill—there's usually confusion or fuzziness before you begin to understand and gain clarity. The same can be true for recognizing and accepting your manifested love.

It's even more challenging if you haven't had positive, successful love relationships as examples to draw from. The only real loving relationships I witnessed up close and personal before Rudy and I found each other was that of my grandparents, Eula and Robert Jones—my mother's adoptive parents—and the Huxtables on *The Cosby Show*.

I believe most of the children of color in the neighborhood where I lived with my mom likely needed, and benefitted from, *The Cosby Show* as a cultural touchstone. Seeing *Doctor* Huxtable and his wife, Clair, an *attorney*, gave way to the idea that both parents could be present in the home, happy together, with successful careers… and they could have fun!

The inspirational portrayals carried over to the college spinoff, *A Different World*, offering a generation whose parents probably hadn't attended or graduated from college a glimpse into academia and dorm life.

I, for one, dreamed of attending a college like Hillman in *A Different World*. The show opened my eyes to what was possible. I even fantasized about how I would decorate my dorm room and which classes I would take. I am thankful to have been able to see that dream realized through our children, as I never experienced it for myself.

As for my grandparent's relationship, they were together from the time my grandmother was 17 until the day that she transitioned, some 55 plus years later. My grandfather ultimately joined her in spirit a few years later. For him, life on earth without his Eula Lee was unbearable. He was 82 when he crossed.

Aside from their illuminated love that gave me hope, when I was a kid, I'd witnessed everything from verbal and physical abuse to cheating. You name it, I probably saw it.

During my formative years, my mother was married to my brother's father. Though I don't remember ever seeing him hit her, I vividly recall a time when he was absent from the house, and she sported a shiner.

I also remember, with the innocence of a child, looking on, as one of my uncles beat his girlfriend right in front of us. They were living with us at the time. I couldn't have been more than eight or nine. I can still see her being pushed up against a dresser in their bedroom and him holding her there with one hand while striking her with a black leather belt with the other. She fought back, but ultimately there were no winners of that round.

It was Bedlam; there was always some type of drama.

Of course, I don't think any of the adults realized how much they were imprinting on us children. I doubt it was even a thought.

I may not have had many positive examples of what love *should* look like growing up—aside from my grandparents, TV shows and fairy tales—but as I got older, what I did know for certain was that I loved myself enough to be *happier alone* than to say yes to anyone who put their hands on me.

The situation with Don was more than enough for me to know that to be true. I would not subject myself—nor my daughter—to any of it.

And neither should you.

You were not put on this planet to be a receptacle for someone else's anger or pain.

Many studies indicate that people who have had unhappy or traumatic childhoods struggle to be happy as adults because it doesn't *feel* right.

According to a 2022 article by Beth Ellwood for *Psypost.com*, a psychology and neuroscience website, a cross-cultural study conducted by Moshen Joshanloo, an associate psychology professor at Keimyung University in South Korea "suggests that people can be afraid of happiness." It's almost as though happiness is not in their *comfort zone*.

This aligns with the psychological concept of *repetition compulsion*, which explains why we tend to recreate the dynamics we observed in childhood, even when they are harmful.

As Olivia Guy-Evans notes in her 2023 Simply Psychology article, *Repetition Compulsion: Why Do We Repeat the Past?*, this self-destructive cycle "can involve people continuously putting themselves in a situation they know is not healthy, perhaps without even realizing that they are repeating their past traumas."

We gravitate toward the familiar because it feels safe, not because it serves us. Thinking back to a few of my mother's relationships, I can recall two of her loves that I thought might have made good father figures. She broke up with them both.

I recently asked her about the breakups. She gave me *reasons* why she couldn't see them being the "one" for her, but now I question, was that because, aside from Eula and Robert, she didn't quite know what love looked or felt like—or even believe that she was worthy of it?

I longed for love and a home filled with warmth similar to what I experienced under my grandparents' roof. I'm sure that's what led me to interior design and real estate—I wanted to *create* the sense of *home* that I didn't fully experience as a child.

We learn about love and relationships through our parents or whoever was present in our lives as we developed. Whether what we observed was good, bad, or indifferent, those experiences become our ingrained examples of love. They shape the way we choose partners and navigate intimacy—often without us even realizing it. They lead us down familiar but unhealthy paths.

To recognize love in a new way—the way you *manifested* it—may not feel right initially if you've never known a love like it before. Accepting it can be challenging and even a bit intimidating, as it may feel as though it is going against the grain.

But sometimes, recognizing and embracing love means trusting the unfamiliar, navigating unexpected paths and in some cases, finding your way back to it—even after years apart.

I recently sat and spoke with Lonnie and Lisa, proprietors of a local family-owned and operated restaurant in Rockland County. They had been married for 14 years—the first time. After a six-and-a-half-year separation, they got back together in 2020.

Lonnie and Lisa grew up with similar traditional family values… and traumas. Both experienced their parents fighting, one a little, the other a lot, though they believed their parents genuinely loved each other. As with many old-fashioned family dynamics, their mothers took care of the house and kids, while their fathers worked (and occasionally played) outside the home.

"I think you're aware that men have affairs. A lot of men have girlfriends on the side while their wives are home," Lonnie shared, reflecting on what he observed growing up. He paused as if he were waiting to see if I would acknowledge his blanket statement. I asked if he knew about the girlfriends during his formative years. Lonnie admitted, "When I got older, I was aware of it, but not when I was a kid."

Growing up in a very social restaurant scene, along with his childhood conditioning, I started to get a deeper insight into the challenges he and Lisa faced in their marriage. Our subsequent conversations only reinforced that understanding.

Lisa added, "[Lonnie] said to me at one point when we were first together, 'I never had anybody love me the way you do.' It was like he was almost annoyed by it."

Lisa's love and affection wasn't what Lonnie was used to.

"I couldn't even understand it myself," Lisa admitted.

I questioned, "Was the love smothering?"

Lisa paused, then continued, "It may have been for him. He was a loner. He likes to be alone. He likes to be in his house."

Lonnie concurred. "I stayed by myself. I'd work and go home. I'd flirt and go on a date every once in a while."

Thinking back to when Rudy and I first started living together, Rudy moved into my South Ozone Park apartment in Queens before we eventually transitioned to Rockland County. His previous independent living experience was limited to staying at home with his mother and brother, and living in a dorm with his five roommates while attending Fordham University as an undergrad.

Rudy's parents divorced and his father left the family home when he was around nine years old. Despite the familial disconnect, Rudy's parents have remained cordial to this day—though I suspect they weren't as cordial immediately following the divorce.

I, on the other hand, had been living on my own since the age of 17. I spent the first two years of Tiera's life with her in Detroit before moving to New York to create a life for us. During that time, I traveled back and forth to spend time with my little girl. It wasn't ideal, but it was the only way I could see to eventually bring us together. Tiera moved with me permanently when she was five.

Tiera's early years mirrored my own experiences growing up. My brother and I lived with our grandparents while our mom worked and attended school. On Fridays, we'd spend the night at her house, returning to our grandparents on Saturday afternoon to prepare for church on Sunday.

We moved in with our mother permanently when I was in fifth grade. We continued spending the weekends with our grandparents on the West Side, with an occasional weekend at *Big Mama's house*. (Big Mama was my mother's biological mom, whom she reconnected with in her early twenties).

Reflecting on how much life changed for Rudy and me, it's amazing how far we've come—from navigating life on my own terms to sharing it with someone else. At that time, I was 28, with this new life partner. Adapting to our new norm, I had my moments of doubt. I laugh now thinking about that time, but there was definitely an adjustment period.

Why does he love me so much?
Why does he want to be so close to me?
Personal space, please! LOL!

Now, with the lack of personal space I give him, especially when we're sleeping, you'd never think that was something I ever had an issue with. How dare I!

I wasn't used to anyone doting over me in the way Rudy did. Most of my previous relationships were about me *proving* myself. I felt as though I had to be the prettiest, dress the coolest, and be accepted by my boyfriend's peers.

With Rudy, I tease that because he was my "*buddy with benefits,*" I could be more laid back—I could be myself.

I allowed Rudy to see the crust in my eyes when I woke up in the morning, and he was privy to the fact that I actually farted... roses of course. But I didn't feel the need to hide it. It was more like, "This is who I am. Take it or leave it." And he loved it.

Our time together was, and always has been so calm and drama-free. Rudy was so attentive that it felt unfamiliar to me. I realize now that what I felt was a shift, and when it finally settled in, there was no doubting it was right.

If you let it, fear can literally rob you from the reality you want to create. If the main qualities you specified for your ideal partner are there, but others are presented in ways you wouldn't have initially gone for—if they are just *different* and not harmful, go for it! And enjoy the ride.

CHOOSING THE PATH OF LOVE

Recognizing love and overcoming fear to realize love when you have it is one thing. Choosing the path of love is an entirely different story.

Imagine going to the grocery store, standing in the produce section, searching for the pineapple. You steer your cart over to the neatly stacked display of tropical treats. You pick one up. You press on it, thump it, sniff it... You might decide to put it in your cart, or you may put it back and select another. There may be nothing wrong with the one you didn't choose, but for whatever reason, you decided it wasn't the one for you—and that's okay. You have the freedom to choose.

Now, just because you selected it doesn't mean that when you cut it open, it will be the sweetest of the bunch. That may have been the one you put back on the display, but again, it's your choice. Choosing love, though similar, isn't quite like selecting produce—it doesn't just sit there, waiting for you to decide.

Love is a mutual choice. You can choose a love, but that love must also choose you back. Real love happens when two people actively and continuously pick each other. It's in the staying, the growing, and deciding over and over again to hold on. Recognizing and choosing love can feel like an abstract concept until you witness it in real life. I was reminded of this idea recently when a dear friend Kendra shared her love story.

Kendra started seeing Dave, who appeared to be perfect for her. She and Dave met on a popular dating site, and their connection, from what she shared, totally reminded me of the way things began with Rudy and me.

Dave was wonderful to Kendra, and it seemed like they were really having a great time together. Kendra confessed that, although she enjoyed Dave's company, she couldn't *see* him being the one.

I also knew she was distracted by a seven-year-plus on-again, off-again relationship with Trevor, a narcissist who she couldn't seem to just walk away from. For over seven years, Kendra found herself entangled in empty promises of engagement, followed by endless excuses as to why Trevor couldn't commit.

To outsiders, her decision to stay was baffling. Kendra's beautiful, smart, talented—any man would be fortunate to be chosen by her. Yet the fear of losing Trevor was so great that she let him back in again and again... and again. Trevor became Kendra's habit. But he hadn't completely chosen her back.

Their relationship seemed to be one of convenience (for him). It was as though she were his *toy*. Trevor would *play* with her for a while, then put her on a *shelf* when he got bored. He would go on long guy trips, as though he were single, and after some time, he would come back to *play* with her again. To avoid moving closer to commitment, he would make up excuses to break up and then come back because he *missed* her.

Disillusioned by his magnetism and charm, she couldn't see the truth about their relationship—until the day she decided she was ready for clarity. It was time to take off the blinders once and for all. Kendra asked the Universe for a sign.

You can receive signs as to whether the relationship you're in is right for you and if it will lead you to the outcome you desire—if (and only if) you choose to accept them.

One of the many ways the Universe communicates to us is through the people around us—family and friends who love and want nothing but the best for us. But the messages don't always have to be from someone close; sometimes, they arrive from unexpected sources. It could be a conversation overheard in a restaurant, or a post shared in a Facebook community group.

The Universe works in mysterious ways.

Now, don't get me wrong. I'm not suggesting you should always listen to others—it depends on their motivation. And remember, you're the one in the relationship with your partner, not your mother. But if you keep hearing the same message from everyone around you, it very well may be a sign—a confirmation that it's time to pay attention.

When Rudy and I were just hanging out as *friends*, I remember talking about him with one of my exes, who remarked, "That Rudy sounds like a really good guy for you. You better take a long, hard look at that one."

Yes, I am still friends with a few of my exes—we just weren't meant to be together in an intimate relationship. Rudy is secure enough with himself and our relationship not to be fazed by them. In fact, Rudy has met a few of my exes, and we've all even gone out to dinner on occasion. Similarly, Rudy has a few female acquaintances that both he and I are friendly with, and they are absolutely wonderful.

When it came to my thoughts about Rudy as my life partner, it wasn't just my ex who made me reflect on the depth of our connection—my mother noticed it too. One night, over a *mother-daughter* dinner at Pizzapapolis in Detroit, complete with deep-dish seafood pizza and a nice bottle of merlot, I opened up to her about the two suitors in my life.

There was Phillipe, another version of the same type of guy I'd always gravitated toward and then there was Rudy—so unlike anyone I dated before him. He was genuinely interested in me and my hopes and dreams. Our time together wasn't just focused on his desires and goals, as with my previous relationships.

My mom listened intently, and when I was done, she leaned back and said, "I don't know about that Phillipe, but you speak about Rudy with passion." It struck me because she never said anything like that about anyone I'd dated before.

Looking back, my mother's words were just one piece of the puzzle. Sometimes the Universe sends us exactly what we need to hear through the voices of those closest to us. Other times, it communicates with subtle signs that can easily be missed if we're not paying attention—or via more obvious signals we might choose to ignore if we're not yet ready to accept the truth.

The idea of signs resonated with me deeply, and it turned out to play a pivotal role in Kendra's journey as well.

Kendra eventually decided to put Mr. Wonderful (Dave) back on the shelf and give her habit, Trevor another shot. This time, however, she asked the Universe for a very specific sign once and for all: Kendra asked for an elephant—she wanted to see an elephant if Trevor wasn't the right partner for her.

Kendra recounted to me that shortly after she asked for this clear directive—less than a week later—she tripped over a small garden statue upon entering a local home goods store. "When I looked down to see what it was, it was a freaking elephant!" Brushing off the clear and very direct sign, Kendra rationalized, "Elephants are a popular home accessory. It has to be a *coincidence*." At least that's what she wanted to believe—until she walked down aisle 7. There Kendra found nothing but wall to wall shelves filled with elephants. I know you're probably thinking, "No way!" But I am here to tell you—yes way! This really happened! And it gets even better.

Believe it or not, even after the aisle of elephants, Kendra *still* talked herself out of accepting the answer given to her so brilliantly from the Universe. Kendra went on to share, "About a month or so after the home store incident, I threw a surprise birthday party for Trevor at my house and his sister walks in saying, 'Here! This is for Trevor'—she proceeds to plop down this nine-inch high, hand carved, silver plated elephant statue on my kitchen counter. Kenyatta! I kid you not. And get this! It was the same exact elephant I tripped over that day in the store. Can you believe it?"

And to make the sign even more significant, Trevor left the statue there for Kendra to see every day—until the time came that she finally accepted the Universe's gesture as the sign she requested and told her habit goodbye for good. *"And take your elephant with you!"*

Signs and the paths we choose go hand and hand.

Think about the world we live in—you can't go down the street without seeing a street sign or a directional marker, nor can you enter a building without noticing one. Beyond the address itself, there are EXIT signs, bathroom signs, room numbers, stair, and elevator indicators… Signs are everywhere.

And that's exactly what it's like in the spiritual realm. We are given signs to help guide us, and they can come in many forms—through a person, a place, spoken or written words… or even an elephant.

As you navigate the path of love and try to interpret the signs along the way—when you reach that fork in the road where you need to decide which direction to move in—block out all of the external noise from your day-to-day life and look within. *Feel* which direction will lead you to where you ultimately want to be.

Ask yourself a series of questions:

- **Does this relationship elevate me?**
- **Do I feel loved and supported?**
- **Are we on the same page as far as where we see this relationship going?**
- **Is this relationship more work than it should be?**

Don't get me wrong—all relationships require some amount of work, but if the work is to actualize the relationship itself, I support your choosing another path.

In Kendra's case, after being in the same relationship with the same person for so many years, there had been more than enough time to move things forward if that were the ultimate goal for both parties.

Instead, they remained stuck in a vicious cycle:

"I love you. I want us to be together. I can't do this because…"

Break up. Miss each other. Get back together.

"I love you. I want us to be together."

You've already been there, done that.

No, this pattern won't change. In order to experience something different, you have to do something different. Don't let your fear of losing something mediocre overpower your desire to achieve something extraordinary. Choose the path of love.

Reflecting on Kendra's Mr. Wonderful, I, too, had a perfectly good love that I shelved. But at only 19 years old, I was way too young and definitely not mature enough to settle down. My ex-husband and I were together for about a year before we had the marriage annulled.

Shortly after, I embarked on a series of dramatic and dead-end relationship experiences, from which I was able to define what I truly desired in a life partner.

There were times along those interim rocky relationship rides, I wondered if I'd made the right decision by leaving my ex-husband. But going back wouldn't have aligned with the future I envisioned for myself, only prolonging the inevitable. My ex-husband and I were never meant to be forever, though I am grateful for the role he played and the connection we shared. I had to keep moving forward.

When Tiera was born, her father was incarcerated. I wanted my daughter to have a grounded and stable home life. Coming from a fairly religious background, my mother didn't approve of my living with a man I wasn't married to, though she didn't lead by example.

"*Shacking up*," the church folk called it. To appease my mother, and give Tiera a present father figure, I did what seemed like the most logical thing to do at the time... I got married.

Shortly after our nuptials, I had a life changing moment while driving to Marygrove College, where I was a student. It was an *aha* moment, if you will—prompted by random thoughts that nagged at me, like a woodpecker persistently pecking at a tree on an otherwise peaceful, crisp spring morn.

I was idled at a traffic light when the question surfaced: *Is this really my life?* I could see the full picture clearly from where I sat. *Married, living in Detroit, with kids—and that's it?*

No exploration? No travel?

The questions echoed within. I wanted more and didn't want to continue on the current route. This realization terrified me. That's when I knew I had to get out—out of Detroit, out of the marriage, and out of the life that wasn't meant to be mine.

I picked up a notepad from the bookstore on Marygrove's campus and began devising my escape plan. I researched fashion merchandising schools, modeling agencies and strip clubs in New York, Chicago, Florida, and Atlanta.

Between securing representation with a boutique modeling agency and landing a position at a Midtown Manhattan strip club, everything came together seemingly seamlessly. The path to the Big Apple was clear. It felt as if New York rolled out the red carpet in anticipation of my arrival. Choosing love for myself, my daughter, and our future, I knew I had to leave. Within a few short months, I was gone.

My then-husband was super supportive of my move to New York, though he believed I'd come back or invite him to join us. But the Mitten State wasn't for me at that time, and neither was he.

The life I left behind may have been enough for some people, and there is absolutely nothing wrong with that. But for me, it was unsettling. The restlessness I felt was like the Universe speaking directly to me. The noise in my head made it unmistakable—it was a definite sign. I was meant to do, see, and experience something different.

Sometimes I reflect on the societal programming we've all been exposed to (thankfully, it's beginning to change). When I was growing up, the expectation for little girls was often to get married, live in a house with a white picket fence, and raise a gaggle of kids. But what about happiness? Shouldn't happiness and self-love be prioritized?

Whether or not you choose to share your life with someone else is entirely up to you—but true love and happiness should resonate within your core before committing to sharing it with another. As a real estate broker, I'm all about picket fences and houses, but without love and happiness within its walls, houses are just lifeless structures.

～

What is the Universe saying to you when you silence the noise of the world and truly tune in to listen? Are you moving along the route that will lead to your wishes come true? Do you feel as though something is just not right with your current situation or path?

I know I've referenced "searching your soul" a few times throughout this journey—tapping into self, going within, essentially, meditating. This internal exploration is a journey in itself and a vital step in guiding you toward true love and the life you desire.

It may take time to feel comfortable with it, but I encourage you to commit to this inner reflection. Once it becomes a habit, you'll discover it to be one of the most powerful tools to assist you in navigating your love and life paths. Some of the best insights often come when you take time to reflect in solitude. Try doing it in the morning before you start your day or in the evening as you wind down.

Consider taking a walk in the woods—not on a dark, isolated path, but during the day—with a friend or even man's best friend if you happen to have a fur baby. "*Come on Max, let's go!*"

Initially, the idea of soul-searching might seem challenging, especially if you're not used to taking time to tap into *self*. Maybe you've never considered meditating at all. But it's through self-reflection—this journey within—that you can begin to understand who you are and what you truly want and need to flourish.

Gateways to assist you on this self-explorative journey are everywhere. Let's take the great outdoors, for instance. There is something about being in nature that almost compels you to delve inward. Look at the trees—how perfectly the branches sway with the wind. Listen to the rustling of the leaves as they gently brush against one another remaining separate yet together, clearing your mind just enough for you to hear… you.

Take a stroll along a beach, observe the shimmering waves of the ocean as they reflect the sun's brilliant glow. Ground yourself—digging your toes in the cool sand—or in the soft grass beneath your feet. Let your eyes follow the horizon as it stretches infinitely before you.

Can you see a picture of your life?
Inhale—Take a deep breath.
Hold it for three counts. Look deeper.
Exhale. Can you see the big picture?
Yes, the one that makes your heartbeat faster when you envision it.
That's the one!
***Feel* the vision.**
Draw it closer to you.
Take in the beautiful sunrise or sunset and embrace the natural cycle

of the sun as it fades away, out of sight as the moon appears, offering light in the midst of darkness. Observe the stars and how they align in the night sky, creating beautiful constellations that spark your imagination. It may not happen right away, though it can. Just keep going.

You will find answers and peace in nature, or even with nature itself.

Take a trip to your local aquarium. One of my favorite activities is zoning out watching jellyfish or observing belugas as they swim playfully. Both sea creatures are so wonderfully tranquil. Shifting your focus from yourself to these serene beings can help quiet the external noise, creating space for you to hear your inner voice.

I absolutely love the eight-foot-tall cylindrical glass display of jellyfish at the Maritime Aquarium in Norwalk, CT. The moon jellies glide through the water capsule so peacefully, like transparent pulsing hearts—beating and floating gracefully together. Each on its own life's mission., quietly colliding yet moving in sync—so poetic and mesmerizing.

Beluga whales with their fun bubble-shaped bodies and playful sounds, evoke pure joy, making you feel lighter and happier. When you come from a place of joy, it can become easier to see a clearer, more positive path. Your mind is open to more possibilities than obstacles and your perception shifts. Joy quiets fear and allows you to engage with life and love from a higher emotional state.

It's hard to make sound decisions from a negative state of mind—whether you're feeling angry, sad, anxious, or depressed. When these overwhelming emotions take over, they tend to cloud your judgement and make everything feel more difficult. But when you find moments of joy and happiness, it's as if the fog lifts, revealing a clearer and brighter path forward.

In a 2015 article by Jennifer S. Lerner, *Emotion and Decision Making*, researchers found that "incidental emotions pervasively carry over from one situation to the next, affecting decisions that should, from a normative perspective, be unrelated to that emotion." This process, known as **carryover of incidental emotion,** explains how anger triggered in one setting can unconsciously create a motive to blame others in unrelated situations. The kicker? This emotional carryover typically happens without us even realizing it's taking place.

But what if you're not into nature? If watching fish *flounder* and venturing in the woods with the possibility of encountering spiders and other creepy crawlers isn't your thing, a visit to a local museum could be just as enriching.

Rudy and I love nature, but we also enjoy the Museum of Natural History, where you can marvel at the remains of a mammoth and the towering skeletal remains of a Tyrannosaurus Rex. One of his favorite exhibits is the Milstein Family Hall of Ocean Life, a two-story gallery dimmed to mimic the depths of the ocean.

Exploring these public resources can offer a surprising escape and perhaps save you some money on therapy. I'm not suggesting these visits replace your professional counsel, but sometimes all you really need is a little time alone—something outside of your routine—to tap into self to analyze what's really going on. Combine this with regular journaling, you should be able to get a better understanding of you and what you need from yourself and your *iron love*.

And if none of these options feel quite right for you, remember this: My first soulful wakeup call came while driving alone.

Be mindful of your thoughts in those seemingly mindless moments—whether you're in the shower, washing dishes, or sitting behind the steering wheel. Often, the clearest answers and brightest ideas surface when you're engaged in solitary, every day, autopilot activities.

Anytime you can spend alone with your thoughts can help you find direction and clarity, so:

- Turn that TV off.
- Log off the computer.
- Turn off the radio.
- Put your phone on silent—better yet, turn it off.

Be completely *present*. Focus on discovering more about you—what you want, what you need, and what love truly means in your life.

Because here's the truth: it's not enough to simply recognize love. You must consciously *choose* the path that leads to it. Along that path, there may be bumps—but there will most definitely be signs. Quieting the noise within creates space for those signs to appear. It allows your own truth to rise to the surface. When we sit with our thoughts, free from the distractions of the outside world we begin to hear the gentle whisper of what we truly want and need. It's in that stillness that clarity emerges. And it's in that clarity that we begin to make choices that *align* with the love we seek. Because choosing the path of love requires more than a fleeting feeling—it requires awareness. It requires courage. And it requires intention.

When you are grounded in yourself, the signs that once seemed subtle begin to shine like guiding lights. The Universe is always communicating, but only in the stillness can we hear. And so, the journey inward becomes the very thing that leads us forward:

Toward love.
Toward truth.
Toward the life we are meant to live.

COMMITTING TO LOVE

When I say, "committing to love", I mean making a conscious decision to move forward in the direction of love. Once you decide you're ready for a loving relationship, it's no longer "I".

Rudy will concur—when I say "*I*", it really means "*we.*" Actually, probably more accurately, it's like when I say, "*we'll* take care of it", that often means *he will*. There's always some variation of "*I*" that is really "*we*" or "*we*" that could mean one or the other. But it's all the same to me—us—or, should I say, *we?* This may well be a running joke amongst committed couples.

Committing means surrendering, the giving of your whole self to another. It *doesn't mean* abandoning your *own* dreams and desires because you're part of a union. True commitment means your partner's dreams begin to blend with yours, and yours with theirs. That's the beauty and the power of real unity.

You're committed to achieving your goals together, and supporting each other through the process. When I think of the synergy of a true, loving relationship, I visualize it as a bird's mating dance.

Each feathered fellow, its own entity, spreading its wings, soaring above the clouds, then choosing to come together as one. They connect, creating this complete and very special moment to bring about procreation, yet able to fly freely, maintaining their own independent self—the perfect unity.

When Rudy and I first got engaged, it was easy for me to say *goodbye* to my other suitors. I was very happy to be moving forward with a man who *everything was easy* with, but what *was* a challenge was saying goodbye to the club. I had worked in strip clubs from the age of 17 until after I met Rudy at 28.

The music, the lights, the pole, the smoke machine and stale cigarette smell (before cigarettes were banned), the countless costumes, the stilettos, the money… It was challenging to walk away.

There was that *fear* again. The fear of falling back into someone's arms and letting them lead, especially since I had been the *Mistress of my Universe* since I was a kid, without anyone else to answer to (with the exception of Tiera's babysitters).

When Rudy and I got engaged, I proudly wore my ring everywhere, including work. I didn't pretend that I wasn't in a *committed relationship*, though I held onto my independence, and kept dancing as my security blanket.

What if things didn't work out? What if something went wrong? The thought of starting over again was terrifying. I'd done that before—surrendered to a possessive love who later told me he couldn't see a life with me and my little girl. He wanted *me*, but my baby and I were a package.

I lost a lot trusting that relationship. The breakup was a horrible experience. Yet again, there *were signs*. I ignored them. We argued. He was extremely jealous and insecure. He was a trust fund baby. The only boy—the family jewel. His family did not like the idea of sharing him with me.

It was all good when we were just *having fun*, but when he showed signs of wanting to take it further, there was an *intervention*. The family as a whole changed face and demeanor, but again, I *knew*, but I allowed myself to fall into it anyway.

Having PTSD from that experience, there was fear to greet me at the door when Rudy and I committed. I wanted to be in it 100%, but I also wanted to have my safety net.

You can't have one foot rooted in faith and the other in fear.

One night while working at Lace, I sat at the bar with John, a *regular*, shooting the shit and drinking. A regular is someone who comes into the club regularly that you can count on for dances, drinks and or money to sit and keep him company while they watch the performances on stage (or the game on TV). Regulars were the best.

I didn't hustle for dances as much after our engagement. I sought after patrons who really just wanted someone to talk to. One of my many super powers, if there is any *one* thing I can do, it's talk.

It feels like yesterday whilst sitting at the bar, John turned to me and said, *"What are you still doing here?"* I looked up at him, confused by his question.

"It's gotta be tough for Rudy that you're still here."

As I could separate my work from home life very easily, I hadn't considered Rudy's *feelings* on the matter. I mean, it is where we met. He knew it came with the territory.

That night after my shift, I asked Rudy how he felt. "I don't like it," he shared. "But I figured you would let go when you were ready."

Ugh! I thought. I really wanted us to work. I didn't want to do anything to jeopardize the success of our relationship, so I committed to making us a priority and made adjustments to make it work… I quit.

It was really one of the hardest things I've ever had to do, but as the saying goes, "Everything you want is on *the other side* of your comfort zone." I wanted to show Rudy that I was committed to making us work. I eventually landed a job as a designer/furniture salesperson at a high-end furniture showroom in Manhattan. It was a lot less pay, but I adjusted… until the day I would decide to get back into real estate.

Committing to love can be challenging. Sometimes it requires us to *shed* old skins—old habits, in order to allow for new love to take root. Adjustments may be needed on both sides. And the more they are communicated, the easier it becomes to incorporate it into your lives.

※

It can be damaging and extremely exhausting to give of yourself wholeheartedly without feeling that your partner is equally committed. It is impossible to perform the dance without a willing and able dance partner.

Take Kendra's 7-year saga for example. She was fully committed to the relationship, but Trevor was not. His lack of commitment led to her frustration and feelings of insecurity. If there is a constant sense of unfulfillment in the relationship, it may be time to reconsider.

If you are truly being honest with yourself, you probably already know whether you and your partner are on equal footing. If one person in the relationship is not committed, or isn't mentally ready or emotionally prepared to commit, the relationship will grow stagnant, and those individual and shared goals will go unfulfilled. Assuming there are shared goals. Because if one person is not truly committed, they may not be able to *see* beyond the end of the block, let alone something five or ten years down the road.

That's why I emphasize the importance of being ready in mind and heart. It's incredibly difficult for anyone to show up fully in love or move a relationship forward if they haven't embarked on the necessary inner work. That includes building self-confidence, developing genuine self-love, learning how to love their partner in a healthy way, and understanding their greater purpose—not just in the relationship, but in life. Without that foundation; that *prework,* love often gets lost in confusion, insecurity or unmet expectations.

As we evolve, there is always work to be done. We are human, after all, and recognizing and owning where we are—and where growth is needed—is all a part of the process. This is why it is paramount to recognize not only where your relationship stands, but also where you are in terms of your own personal growth, before committing fully to iron love.

Pay attention to the words you and your partner use when speaking to one another. Do you hear *"we"* and *"us"* when discussing future plans, or is it more *"I"* and *"me"*? You've probably heard a thousand times that communication is the key to all relationships—it's especially true when it comes to matters of the heart. It's not just about how we speak; it's also what's being said. What words do you use when describing your relationship? What words do your partner use? Do they reflect commitment? Or hint at hesitation? Communication is how we exchange information—through symbols, signs, behaviors, words… and even silence. Oh yes, silence can speak volumes.

When committing to a loving relationship, you're essentially saying, "I am giving you all of me." And in giving your all, you should feel confident that your partner is giving the same in return. This is the foundation of iron love.

Whether you're trying to decide if you should continue on the path of your current relationship or if you're already in an established relationship that may be having a rough go, there is no way to truly know where you stand without clear communication.

You can *feel* when someone is truly into you or if your partner is currently distracted by something else—you will be the best gauge. Reading the energy that your loved one emits will tell you everything you need to know about where your partner is in the moment and even within the relationship. We're not just talking about the energy felt when you are having a good time. Does the energy shift when you discuss things like commitment or a future together? Or is your partner's energy the same no matter the topic of conversation?

My energy definitely shifted the night Rudy told me about his prospective date. I sat in the passenger seat of his black Nissan Ultima, staring out the window to avoid eye contact at all cost. The only sound heard was the white noise coming from outside the car as we drove down the highway. The air was thicker than the gravy grandma made to go with her roast on Sunday afternoon. With my arms folded, I completely shut down. There is no doubt Rudy could *feel* something was wrong.

Energy can be like a magnet—repelling and attracting. When you're with your partner, if the connection feels off, or you sense a subtle pull away instead of toward, your body (or theirs) may be sending a clear message that the connection needs to be reestablished.

- *Does your partner avoid eye contact?*
- *Is he or she constantly distracted by social media, the news or YouTube?*
- *Does she or he seem to be easily annoyed?*

All could be signs for a need to reconnect. In reconnecting, it's important to analyze the bigger picture to fully understand what's really going on. Try to approach the situation with empathy for your significant other. See the world through your partner's eyes. Is he or she tired or overwhelmed? If so, now may not be the best time to communicate. Be patient and wait until your partner is well-rested and in a better state to connect effectively.

If you are in a committed relationship and your significant other is experiencing additional stress at work, allow them some space to openly share with you. This is not to say that you wouldn't give the same courtesy to someone you are newly dating, but at the same time the level of invested energy will be different for someone you're just seeing versus someone you're committed to.

Ask if he or she is looking for solutions or just wanting to vent. Making room for this openness is a lesson I've had to learn over the years—and one I still work on. Yes! I still actively work on it. Just because Rudy and I have a wonderful, loving relationship doesn't mean that it's as good as it can be.

Reflecting on my role as a real estate broker, I thrive on solving problems for my clients and my team members. However, when Rudy shares with me, sometimes he'd just like me to listen—not advise. Asking your partner what they want or need ensures you're not unintentionally adding to their stress by trying to help when help isn't what they're looking for. And by all means, when your partner is communicating with you, get rid of all distractions and BE PRESENT.

In addition to the previously mentioned diversions, be sure to sit down and give your undivided attention. Don't try to process the dialogue whilst in the middle of doing household chores or typing your report due tomorrow.

Nothing can shut a person down faster than the feeling of not being heard or understood. When your iron love is ready to share their thoughts, show up with open ears and an open heart—prepared to truly listen.

If your partner isn't yet ready to communicate, don't take it personally or let their dark cloud vibes rain on your good-mood parade. We all have bad days, and your partner's bad days may have absolutely nothing to do with you. Be there for them but allow them space to figure it out on their own. As we evolve, there is always work to be done. We are human, after all, and recognizing and owning where we are—and where growth is needed—is all a part of the process.

֍

It's normal to have some moments of disconnect. Just because you two are in a committed relationship doesn't mean that you will agree on everything. You are individuals who may have come from completely different backgrounds. As you merge your lives, there will inevitably be pieces that fit better than others. In those instances where things don't align perfectly, adjustments may be necessary by one or both parties.

Modifications in habits, ways of thinking and considerations you didn't think about when operating in *"me"* mode are all parts of the evolution. This shift is natural and completely normal. Thinking about my relationship with Rudy over the years, there have certainly been adjustments on both sides—but we don't argue.

Don't get me wrong, we have had some heated discussions over the years. I'm not trying to convince you that we've never been so passionate about our differing opinions that voices weren't raised. My normal tone is speaking as though I'm standing at a podium with a live audience in the room. Yes, I can be loud and quite dramatic when I am excited about something, but this is not arguing.

When I think of an argument, I think of chaos—something without resolution that leads to attacking each other just to prove a point. Rudy and I may see things differently from time to time, but we discuss those differences and work toward a happy medium, ensuring the discussion doesn't remain open-ended.

Once we reach a resolution, we're on the same page—and that's it. On to the next thing. There's no bringing it up again, no rehashing. We discuss, we listen, we make decisions and we move on.

Conflicts in relationships often arise from differences in communication styles. *Conflict styles* as it is described in an April 2025 article, written by Jenna Ryu for *Self.com*, *7 Common Conflict Styles That Show Up in Relationships, According to the Experts*. "Whether you shut down, lash out, or dodge the conversation altogether, your go-to method reveals a whole lot about your communication habits—and, more importantly, what you can do to resolve issues more effectively..."

One person might approach things with logic and reason, while the other leads with emotion. This disconnect can make it feel like progress is impossible, especially when both individuals feel unheard or misunderstood. Balancing conflict styles and communicating effectively in a relationship comes down to choosing to be understanding, being able to adapt, and express intentionally. During particularly challenging times, it's important to pause and ask yourself how you're contributing to the dynamic.

When tensions are high, trying to push through with your usual way of communicating can sometimes feel like pouring gasoline on a fire. Instead, consider taking a step back and asking the Universe, or simply using your own intuition, for guidance. Visualize the outcome you want—connection, understanding, peace. Focus on what that looks and feels like, and let that intention guide your next steps.

When you do engage, truly listen to your partner. Read between the lines of what they are saying. Acknowledge their pain and take accountability for your part in the conflict. It takes two to tango. Whether consciously or unconsciously, both individuals play a role in the breakdown of a relationship.

If your relationship is in a state of constant disconnect, it doesn't necessarily mean it's time to throw in the towel. I love the exercise suggested by Marci Shimoff in Rhonda Byrne's documentary, *The Secret:*

"Even if you're having a really hard time in a relationship, you can still turn that relationship around. Take a piece of paper and for the next thirty days, once a day sit down and write all the things that you appreciate about that person. Think about all the reasons that you love them. You appreciate their sense of humor. You appreciate how supportive they are. And what you'll find is when you focus on and appreciate acknowledging their strengths, that's what you'll get more of, and the problems will fade away."

Now, don't take that the wrong way. It's not just writing out positive things about your loved one. It's about the *emotion* you experience when you focus on those positive affirmations. When you genuinely *feel* grateful and appreciative for someone, your actions, and reactions toward them will reflect that—and that, my friend, is where the magic happens.

I've engaged in a similar practice over the years. Nobody is perfect. Not me, not you and not your significant other. There are going to be things that your partner does that may ruffle your feathers, but how important are they in the scheme of everything?

For example:

- "Ugh! He forgot to take out the garbage... again."

- "Why does she leave her makeup spread out all over the counter?"
- "I wish he would put the dirty clothes in the basket instead of the floor."

Before nagging your partner about these little things, think about the positives their presence brings to your life:

- "He always makes sure there is an amazing home cooked meal waiting for me when I get home from work."
- "I love that she's super handy and takes care of the home repairs."
- "He appreciates and accepts me for who I am."
- "I love how supportive she is with the things I want to do."

Remember, whatever you concentrate on grows. Being mindful of the good your partner brings to the table can be enough to keep negativity at bay. And if you really want to shut *that ego* down, open your eyes and take ownership of your own imperfections. Woo! Now that there is eye-opening!

Committing to love also means committing to seeing yourself for who and where you are... and who you want to become, making a conscious decision to consistently work on your growth for the betterment of your life and your relationship.

Be committed to working through any moments of disconnect no matter if you're the driver, wanting to understand where you are on your journey and where you're going, or sitting in the passenger seat... fogging up the window.

☙

Be careful not to confuse commitment with marriage or weddings. Not everyone's picture of commitment will look or feel the same. Like fingerprints, love and commitment are as unique as the pads on the tips of your fingers. Even if they seem similar, no two relationships will be carbon copies. This is why you should never compare your relationship to anyone else's. Trying to compare diminishes the unique beauty and value that yours holds.

Not to mention, you can never fully know what's happening behind closed doors. What you see is only what the union allows you to see. Focus on your own life and your love. Be happy for others but direct your energy toward nurturing your relationship.

This principle doesn't just apply to relationships—it rings true for all aspects of your life. If you're busy trying to figure out what Sally in the HR department is doing at work, you're diverting energy away from turning your own dreams into reality.

Speaking of weddings and marriages, a couple of years ago our Tiera surprised us with 24-hour notice for her wedding. She and her then fiancé, Luis, had initially planned for October 2023 but later decided they didn't want the stress of a traditional wedding.

During a spring break trip to Florida to visit Luis' family, his grandfather asked, "If you love each other, why wait?" Inspired by his words, the couple decided to say their *"I dos"* when they returned to New York, the couple tried to keep it to themselves, but once the family caught wind of it (and Tiera confirmed) we all adjusted our schedules to be there for the special day.

What followed was a whirlwind of last-minute dress shopping, shared laughter, and a mother-daughter bonding memory I'll cherish for the rest of my days. Tiera said, *"Yes"* to the dress just hours before the ceremony—proof that when you stay open to possibilities, the Universe steps in.

As Rudy and I walked Tiera down the aisle, I held back tears reflecting on how he and I have modeled love and commitment for our family. We've shown that love isn't about perfection but about navigating life's roads together, adapting, and supporting each other along the way. While our children's journeys are their own to experience, I hope our love and the example of our life together serve as a guide for them as to what is possible and what commitment really means.

I began to think about Rudy's and my wedding—a day filled with love, joy, imperfection, and truly unforgettable moments.

When Rudy and I planned our first wedding, (yes, we've married each other twice), I said yes to the first dress I tried on months before our big day. It was off the rack from Brava Boutique, a little bridal shop in Forest Hills, Queens. The dress was adorned with white floral lace appliques and strands of pearls that danced around the silky milk-white fabric. It featured a faux turtleneck with an open back lightly covered with sheer lace, finished with a sweeping mermaid cut that fit like a glove.

Dr. Mark Chapman, Rudy's professor from Fordham University, guided us through premarital counseling and performed the enchanted ceremony before our host of loved ones. Our wedding party consisted of five bridesmaids, five groomsmen, two flower girls, one ring-bearer, and around 150 guests made up of family, colleagues, and our closest friends.

> **Fun Fact:**
>
> Rudy and I married at the Coral House in Baldwin, New York, the same venue I caught my friend Paula's wedding bouquet some five years earlier. I didn't realize it was the same place until a visit while scouting for our wedding location.

The blush floral wallpaper that lined the halls looked awfully familiar. After the tour, I reached out to Paula for verification. She confirmed that Coral House was, in fact, where she wed. We took that as a sign that Coral House was the right place for our special day.

July 15, 2000. Our wedding day. Nothing could be more special—or more eventful.

The day began with torrential rain, delaying our friend Mario's flight into JFK. He was supposed to play guitar and sing Joe Cocker's *"You Are So Beautiful to Me"* as I walked down the aisle, but now he wouldn't make it in time. Adding to the chaos, the beautiful courtyard ceremony we planned in front of nearby Millburn Pond had to be moved inside the venue's dimly lit chapel.

As if that wasn't enough, we soon discovered my veil had accidentally been left behind in Rockland County—over an hour away. Then, while walking from the parking lot to the venue, the tail of my gown slipped out of its protective garment bag and landed in a puddle of mud. And just minutes before the ceremony, my wedding band rolled out of my brother-in-law's hand and disappeared under a piano. Despite all the mishaps, everything came together so magically in the end, as if it was all just meant to be.

Rudy's cousin, Richie was in attendance with his friend, Sara, who just so happened to be an accomplished pianist. Sara played the Joe Cocker tune softly on the very piano my ring rolled under. My uncle Julius walked me down the aisle in the absence of my dad, who passed away seven years prior.

Rudy's aunt Helen, an amazing seamstress, found a stray petticoat left behind by another bride and crafted a beautiful veil of tulle shortly before the ceremony. Prepacked Clorox wipes saved my muddy mermaid tail, and my wedding band was recovered in the nick of time.

Even the sun decided to make an appearance for post-nuptial pictures, and all was right with the world. In fact, there was even a brilliant rainbow spotted in the sky. It turned out to be the most beautiful day, and we were grateful to share it with so many loved ones.

Our second ceremony was *a lot more* intimate. Almost thirteen years later, on the evening of January 26th, 2013, Rudy and I decided to do it again. During the fall of 2012, I worked the *BNRG Power Crunch* booth at *Mr. Olympia* in Las Vegas. When I returned home to New York I told Rudy all about the experience.

"We could actually go during Martin Luther King, Jr. weekend," Rudy suggested. Before we knew it, our mini getaway to Sin City was booked… though we had to sit through a timeshare presentation to make it happen, but we were in! Just before our trip, I took it upon myself to propose to my iron love and this time, he said *yes*.

> **Fun fact:**
>
> As a unique surprise for our weekend getaway, Rudy rented a Porsche 911 for me to test drive through Red Rock. He knew it was on my vision board and wanted me to see what it felt like to press my foot down on the gas pedal. I drove through the canyon with the wind kissing my cheeks at a whopping 70 MPH. (Hey! I was into the shape, not the speed. But seriously, I give credit to the experience for assisting me in manifesting my own Porsche 911 eight years later.)

Rudy and I exchanged vows at the Little Church of the West. I wore a sexy little milk-white, off-the-shoulder cocktail dress I found on the sale rack at Macy's in the Palisades Mall. It was a Jessica Simpson tunic design that cost around $50. I paired it with Pleaser "glass" (plastic) slippers—the same ones I loaned Tiera for her big day *(Her "something borrowed")*.

We briefly toyed with the idea of having an Elvis impersonator perform the ceremony but decided on an ordained minister instead. We didn't want to jinx the day by not taking it seriously, though I'm sure plenty of happily wedded couples have tied the knot under *The King's* supervision. (*Thank you very much*, in my Elvis voice.)

That night, it was the two of us, the minister, and a chapel witness. I called my girlfriend Patricia (aka Patty) for support, holding my mobile in hand while tracing my lips in a chocolate-brown liner with the other. I wished Patty could have been there with me, but her comforting words over the phone was the next best thing. With no stylists on hand, I accepted the roles of makeup artist and hairdresser, determined to look just as radiant for my groom this time as I had the first time around.

As I stood in the dressing room, waiting for our magic hour, I thought about our journey. Here we were, almost 13 years into our union, fully aware of what marriage entails and what we're each capable of. Knowing all, we were ready to say "yes" to each other again. That's the beauty of commitment—it's not about perfection or grand gestures. It's about choosing each other, over and over, even knowing all the ups and downs that life together can bring.

Even today, I'd still say "yes" to Rudy again in a heartbeat. We've joked about getting married two more times—once for each season—so we'd have extra special days to celebrate. The truth is, whether or not we add more nuptials to our story, every day we wake up next to each other is a gift and reason to celebrate. Sometimes out of the blue, Rudy will look at me and ask, "You wanna get married?" It's his way of saying, "I love you." And my answer, every time, is "Yes."

∽

Whether you choose to marry or not should have no bearing on your love and commitment to one another. That is, unless one of you wants the

Iron Love | 83

tradition and the other doesn't. And if that is the case, it's a conversation worth diving into to ensure you are both on the same page about what you want.

What if neither of you want marriage or children? Marriage doesn't define commitment, nor does the choice to start a family. Babies may tie your DNA together, but procreation doesn't guarantee love, happiness, nor commitment.

Rudy and I have friends who have been together for well over 15 years without ever marrying. Their love and dedication to each other is as strong and enduring as any marriage we've witnessed. They are happy simply being together, and their Iron Love has outlasted countless other marriages.

In exploring perspectives from others, I connected with Susan, a three-time Ironman Triathlon athlete, who's been with her life partner, Jim for 23 years. Jim and Susan met at a bar in the Hamptons almost 25 years ago. That evening, they shared drinks, laughter, and light conversation, but it wasn't until the following year—the same weekend—they met again and recognized their undeniable connection. From that moment on, they didn't let it go.

Their relationship evolved naturally. After some time, Jim moved from his shared rental in New York City into Susan's two-bedroom apartment in Englewood, NJ. There was no formal discussion of marriage. Their partnership flowed naturally without pressure from either side.

"Recently there's been talk of marriage, but for the wrong reasons," Susan stressed when I spoke with her. "I lost my job and needed benefits, and even though we've been together for 23 years, in order for me to be eligible for his benefits, we would actually have to be married. There is no domestic partnership in New Jersey."

Susan further explained that they learned that for her to qualify for his benefits without marriage, they would both have to be 62. "Which seems to me like discrimination." Susan added. "Why do I have to be 62 to get partner benefits?"

The situation didn't seem fair. "But that's not the right reason to get married," she reflected. "Yes, we can go to the Justice of the Peace and get married, but we decided against it."

Susan's clarity about marriage stems from past experience. "I was married before—it barely lasted six months. I knew he was the wrong person before but chalked it up to wedding jitters and went through with the whole wedding... Right after we got married, he started pressuring me to have children right away. And I didn't know if I wanted to have children," Susan paused. "It wasn't something that I *didn't* want, but it wasn't something that I wanted right away."

After about six months, Susan chose to honor the feeling *'This is not what I want.'* "I gave back the ring and moved back home with my mother. I wanted out and I wanted out the best way for me."

Susan left with only her personal belongings, leaving him with their wedding gifts and memories of that day. Shortly after, the marriage was annulled.

And "that was the end of that."

Susan confessed that she was so certain that her ex wasn't the right partner for her that she never changed her name. Although she had gone through the motions of the wedding, Susan admitted she was never truly *committed*. Listening to Susan's story reminded me of my first marriage. When it's not right, instinctively, you know—you feel it. If you're reading this now and a light bulb is going off, your heart is beginning to race, or you're feel-ing a little uneasy because these words resonate with you, it may be time to think about making a change. Take some time alone to reflect and listen to your soul. Refer to pages 65-68 for guidance. Find a place that brings you peace and write out your thoughts and feelings. After you've had some time to step away from it—perhaps a few days—come back to your words. Read them as though they are not your own, but instead like you're an outsider, looking in...

What do you see when you take feelings and emotion out of the situation?

If you don't see fulfillment and a future, it may be time to let it go. And that, my friend, is okay. Life is too short to be miserable. We were put on this planet to feel and experience life and love—not to be perpetually unhappy.

Commit to loving yourself enough to learn from your experiences. Life is a journey of growth, and every misstep, heartbreak, and revelation have the potential to lead you closer to the love and fulfillment you desire. We begin to shape the picture of what we want in life by our experiences. From those, we decide to welcome more of what we like and enjoy and are also able to recognize the things that we don't want. Without the stormy rain clouds, how would we ever fully appreciate the feeling of summer's sun rays caressing our skin during the break of day?

If you are able to pinpoint undesirable patterns, commit to breaking free from them, and making new choices. Learn to develop and trust your instincts, honor your value, and remember you are deserving of a life that brings you joy. Let your past serve as a guide—not a weight—and move forward with the intention to live and love fully.

Commitment transcends wedding vows, family ties and other perceived obligations. It comes from within—a deep, personal drive to keep moving forward, to learn and to grow and never give up. True commitment only falters when one partner isn't truly vested. May you and your iron love share a connection and devotion to yourselves and each other that withstands the test of time.

INCORPORATING LOVE

Togetherness: The uniting of individuals who have committed to moving forward in life as one. Like any other goal or dream, a shared image of what that union looks like and what it means to each participant is essential for it to be obtainable. Without a clear vision, one partner may be painting a Van Gogh while the other uses Michelangelo's brushstrokes. This doesn't mean that the union won't result in a *High Renaissance/Post-Impressionistic masterpiece*, but the ultimate picture may not be as easy to comprehend and may take longer to achieve.

Communicating what you both envision for the relationship—and what you want to work toward for yourselves (together and individually), and the lives of your children should you choose to have them—ensures that your actions align with the master plan.

I've created lists of **Things to do, have and become** for as long as I can remember. It was something I picked up from a personal development workshop my mother participated in while she attended Marygrove College. I sat at a desk in the back of the classroom while the adults took the front seats and actively *worked* on themselves.

The facilitator looked down at me as he walked by my desk. He smiled and handed me a sheet of paper with the aforementioned heading. From that moment on, penning my desires became a regular part of my journey. It was what I did when I decided to move to New York from Michigan. Putting pen to paper is what I did when I decided to give a description to my iron love, and then writing lists became a part of our journey together.

Putting pen to paper is what I was moved to do to share what I've learned with you.

Though I shared my lists with Rudy previously, it wasn't until our 9th wedding anniversary that we began to really focus on *joint goals* in a very intentional way. Yes, we employed this practice to create a plan to pay down debt, affording us the ability to save up the down payment for our first house, but that was just one thing… and then we challenged ourselves.

To celebrate our 9th year together, we booked a wonderful weekend stay at a boutique hotel in New York City's Tribeca—a much needed break away from our obligations (kids, work and housekeeping) to enjoy a few days filled with lots of fun activities. We were amazed by the bird's eye view of Manhattan and her bridges during an epic helicopter ride around the city. We had a relaxing evening at a Wall Street Bath & Spa 88, topped with an awesome massage. We went dancing and crashed a pool party at another hotel midtown. And on our final day, we took part in a super cool trapeze class in Chelsea Piers.

The class had about eight other participants that afternoon, one of which was a girl who took the class as a *bucket list* item. She called it her *Thirty by 30*—thirty things to achieve by the age of 30. *What a neat idea*, we thought. Rudy questioned her about the items on her list. I can't remember any other goals she shared, but trapeze was a lot of fun… and definitely got our adrenaline rushing. For a minute I even considered giving it all up and joining the circus… Ummm and then I thought again.

That weekend was exactly what we needed. We came back recharged and ready to take on the world. Rudy was extremely inspired by the girl's list. So much so, he decided to create a *Forty by 40* list when we returned home. That was the beginning of our list making together.

> **Fun fact:**
>
> *Competing in an amateur bodybuilding competition was originally Rudy's goal. Since it was on his list, when I learned one of my client's friends was competing in a competition, I made it a point to get tickets for us to check out. That was how I met my first bodybuilding coach and began prepping for my first competition, and the rest is herstory.*

When I received my first diet regimen, I was sooooo confused.

Meal 1-Breakfast

- *4 egg whites*
- *15 almonds*
- *1 cup steamed asparagus*

Meal 2 Mid-Morning

- *2 scoops protein powder*
- *1 tablespoon of peanut butter*
- *1 rice cake*

Meal 3 Lunch

- *4 oz chicken*
- *1 cup of steamed broccoli*
- *15 almonds*

How do you just eat 15 almonds? I thought. *How do you measure 4 oz of chicken?* I couldn't comprehend it. At that time I thought eggplant parmigiana was a healthy meal. This food prescription made absolutely no sense to me. I might as well have been trying to read braille.

Rudy, being the partner he is, knew that I was clueless and took my list and got all of the groceries for me to begin prep. It was like the scene from *"The Color Purple"* when Oprah Winfrey's character, Sofia, is forced to work for the mayor's wife, but she can barely read the grocery list. Whoopi Goldberg's character, Ms. Celie sees Sofia struggling. She takes the piece of paper from Sofia and gathers the items from her list. Sometimes you just need a helping hand from a friend… or your iron love. Aside from helping me with my prep, Rudy decided to take the opportunity to cross *bodybuilding* off his list since I would already be meal prepping, and so we embarked on the bodybuilding journey together.

One significant aspect of this joint venture that is worth noting, is although Rudy and I shared the common goal of attaining the best physique possible (for our respective competitions), our methods of achieving the desired results were completely different. The differences reflected not only the physiological distinctions between our bodies, but also the unique ways we approached discipline and training. While I was doing two rounds of cardio almost every day, Rudy's routine included only 20 minutes of light walking every other day. His diet allowed for steak and sweet potatoes, while I found creative ways to enjoy tilapia, asparagus, and the occasional serving of brown rice. Yet, through these different journeys to the same destination, we remained side by side, supporting each other through every phase of the process.

Sharing your goals with your loved one opens their receptors to begin to listen and be on the lookout for opportunities and clues that may help you reach your goal. It puts your desires on their radar. Two brains and four ears can often be more effective than one brain and two eyes (eight if you're like us and wear glasses).

Rudy and I still create our own individual lists and vision boards, but now, in addition to those we have a combined list featuring the things *we* both would like *to do, have and become*. We add to and take away from our list as goals are accomplished or desires shift. (Some ideas change as we evolve.)

As two goal-oriented individuals, what we've learned over the years is that when we focus on the same goals together, whether they are our joint or individual goals, we are able to accomplish them faster. There is absolutely nothing like having your own personal support/cheerleader by your side. I know for certain that we have achieved as much as we have solely because of our togetherness and support for one another.

When we started this iron love journey 25+ years ago, we had no idea what we would or could create. If you recall, one of Rudy's first declarations to me was *"I'm only going to make about $50,000 a year."* Back when we started out, our beliefs were limited by what we knew and *saw* as possible at that time. The more we move forward together, the bigger we are able to dream and create. The more we are able to realize, the more confidence it gives us to try something greater.

We now know that it really isn't that difficult to achieve the things you dream of with focus, effort and persistence. Inevitably we learn something new and grow in the process. The key is you just have to go for it and <u>not let fear</u> get in the way. And so we continue to go for it… and we do it together.

⤸

Love as an Addition, Not a Never-Ending Sacrifice

In a healthy, fulfilling relationship, you shouldn't have to abandon your friends and family, or the activities that bring you joy to please your partner. This new union should be a beautiful addition to your already love-filled life. And I do mean love-filled—even if the only love in your life at the moment is the love you radiate within yourself. *You* have to love *yourself* first.

Years ago I had a dear friend whose husband was so insecure that whenever we went out for girls' night, he would keep tabs to see exactly where we were, what we were up to and who we were with. Overhearing their exchange—it was like she was forever being interrogated. He called so much he might as well have been out with us. It would always lead into an argument. It was the worst! We eventually just stopped going out together. Aside from being subjected to constant questioning, she'd also *transformed* from the fun, independent woman I'd always known to this *Mrs. Cleaver* character (from the 60's TV sitcom *Leave It to Beaver*—I know I'm really aging myself here).

There is definitely a shift when you are in a committed relationship—you may make dinner for two (or more if you have a family) rather than one. You make plans for both or consider your significant other before making independent plans. That shift is one thing, but this was some *Stepford Wives* kind of shift. My girl had turned into a robot, catering to his every need. This was not the person he married; the person I'd been friends with for so many years.

A few years later we discovered the reason he was so into what *she* was doing was because he was actually cheating—projection in action. It's never a good sign when your partner tries to take over your life or accuse you of things you know in your heart you're not doing. When you say *"I do"* you don't become someone's possession. Incorporating love into your life doesn't mean losing yourself—it means maintaining your sense of self while welcoming another person into your world.

The Freedom to Fully Be Yourself

When I first introduced Rudy to some of my friends they could see that we were compatible, but because he was reserved, they assumed he didn't vibe with them, when in fact, it had absolutely nothing to do with them. That's just the way he was to new people. I've often referred to my iron love as the *WB (Warner Bros.) Frog*, though a lot less over the years.

If you don't know the cartoon character, his official name is Michigan J. He was discovered in a metal box near an abandoned building and pops out dancing and singing the catchy 1890's tune, "**Hello! Ma Baby**" by Joseph E. Howard and Ida Emerson. The discoverer, a construction worker, thinks that he will become rich by getting Michigan J. to perform in front of an audience, but when he opens the box, all he gets is *"ribbit."* Some pieces of you should be reserved for your iron love and that's ok. Not everyone should be privy to every bit of you.

With Rudy, I never felt as though I had to impress him or be anything other than my authentic self. There was no pretense. It was the most comfortable I've ever been with anyone outside of my family and closest friends. It was—and still is absolutely wonderful. I want that for you.

The strongest relationships are not about control or jealousy. They're about support and love, built on a foundation that allows each person to be their best self.

Merging Lives with New Outlooks

When Rudy and I first moved in together, I'd been living on my own since I was 17, in *my own* space, making *my own* rules. I came into our relationship with an eight-year-old daughter, whom I'd been raising as a single parent, with tremendous support from my tribe. *(Thank you, Weisy, Dandee, Paula, Joanna, and Mom.)*

Now, here I was in a committed relationship with someone who embraced my child as his own. That embrace came with *his own* ideas of parenting, which weren't always the same as mine. However, through mindful communication, we were able to understand each other's perspectives and surrender to what we collectively decided was the best approach for each situation.

An early example of this occurred during our first Christmas together, just days after Rudy and I got engaged. While shopping at the Palisades Mall, my daughter, Tiera picked up an ornament or some sort of trinket she knew she should not have touched and accidentally broke it.

My initial reaction was, *"Okay, leave it on the shelf and let's go."* Hey, don't judge me—this was a long time ago! Being human, we don't always do the right thing or know what the right thing is until we do. Rudy's response, however, was, *"Tiera broke it. We'll pay for it, and she'll have to pay us back."*

It's incredible when your partner helps you see things from a different perspective, and you're receptive to their point of view. Coming together from different paths means your reactions to situations won't always be the same.

My life's journey before Rudy might have led me to leave the broken pieces on the shelf and kept it moving. Rudy's path, however, emphasized taking responsibility. I recognized his approach as *the right thing to do* in that situation, so we incorporated that lesson into our child-rearing. From then on, whether it involved Tiera or our future children, Rudy and I agreed on how to handle such situations. Even now, as our children transition into adulthood and we navigate our ever-evolving roles as parents and do our part to support our family's growth, these discussions continue.

✦

When people come together as one, it's vital to keep ego in check and recognize that you won't have all of the answers—especially if you truly want the union to work. That is what committing is about. Ego, when unchecked, is an inflated sense of pride or self-importance that places the individual above the partnership. *In a relationship where the goal is to become one, how can ego exist without creating distance?*

Destructive ego thrives on the need to be right, to win, or to protect a fragile sense of self at the expense of harmony. It undermines the life you're trying to build together and can breed animosity, weakening the very core of your connection. More often than not, this kind of ego stems from insecurity—a lack of self-assurance that should be worked on before saying yes to a long-term partnership.

Sadly, I've witnessed many intelligent, accomplished people struggle to sustain togetherness. And for the most part the root of the issue has been an inflated ego. Relationships become more about the individual than the unit, exhibited through public displays of superiority or competition. Confidence, however, is not to be confused with an inflated ego. Confidence allows you to love fully, without fear, and to support your partner without feeling diminished. While confidence can grow within love, both partners must be committed to evolving together.

In pursuit of togetherness, you have to be willing to listen, learn and support your partner wholeheartedly. I want Rudy to achieve everything he desires because what's good for him is good for me and our family. I want him to grow beyond measure because that's what he wants and is capable of—and he supports my hopes, dreams, and desires in the same way. As pillars in our community—Rudy as the superintendent in a high-performing school district and I, the owner of a local boutique real estate brokerage—we've achieved a great deal together, as well as individually.

Sometimes, the spotlight shines solely on one of us. But as a couple, we both draw energy from its rays. When Rudy is in the limelight, if I'm not beside him, I'm behind the lamp, ensuring it highlights his best side. Or I'm the loudest voice in the audience cheering him on. "Rudy! Rudy! Rudy!" And that's the way it should be—a continuous exchange of positive energy, flowing seamlessly from one half of the unit to the other.

Criticizing your partner in front of others can also be a significant relationship killer. If something feels off in your connection, address it privately. Criticism, in any form, can dim your partner's light, leaving them feeling incomplete—like their glass is perpetually half empty—questioning whether you truly love them *as they are*. Publicly embarrassing your partner not only creates discomfort for everyone present but also erodes trust—the cornerstone of any strong relationship.

I recently spoke with an acquaintance, Anna, who ended a 17-year relationship after enduring years of belittling from her partner, often in front of their family, and their young, impressionable children. Nothing she did was ever good enough. It was as though Anna's every move was to try to please him and no matter what she did, she always fell short. The breaking point came when their 13-year-old son began mimicking his father's behavior toward her. "I can't let my son think it's acceptable to treat women that way," Anna shared with me.

Determined to break the cycle of dysfunctional love, Anna made the courageous choice to forge a healthier path for herself and their children. With a resolute heart and newfound sense of freedom, she walked away from the relationship, leaving behind the weight of a love that had long since atrophied.

If your partner is not uplifting you or creating a safe space for love and knocking you down has become the norm, communicate your feelings. Through thoughtful communication, try to get them to see how they are contributing to the erosion of what you once had. Promises to change must be backed by action or you may find yourself in an undesirable pattern that will need to be broken. This is not togetherness.

Trying to build a life with someone you're not aligned with will inevitably lead to challenges, especially if you're striving to live life as your authentic self—and that should be the goal. You should feel the most comfortable being perfectly, imperfectly you with your partner.

Alignment in a relationship is about more than just shared goals—it's about understanding and supporting each other on every level. Togetherness isn't simply mutual respect; it's about showing up for one another every day, choosing to listen, grow, and build something greater than the sum of its parts.

It's about creating a partnership where individuality is celebrated but never at the expense of unity. Aligning your visions, supporting one another's dreams, and always working toward a shared purpose are key. This kind of connection doesn't happen by chance—it requires intentionality, vulnerability, and a commitment to nurturing the relationship.

When couples achieve this level of alignment, they create a bond that transcends the ordinary. It becomes a union that uplifts both partners, inspiring them to be their best selves while standing strong against the challenges of time. Togetherness isn't just a foundation; it's the essence of a relationship built to last. An *Iron Love* relationship.

Sometimes, in the name of togetherness, you may choose to make sacrifices that seem to be beneficial for the relationship but come at the expense of your personal or professional growth. I caution against these kinds of sacrifices, as they can ultimately stunt both your and your partner's development, becoming a breeding ground for resentment over time. When our boys were young (just six and three) Rudy was still early in his career in education. He worked as a social studies teacher and served as the department chair at Nyack High School. Even then, his leadership potential was undeniable. Anyone paying attention could see he was poised for more.

Then an opportunity arose. The principal at the high school was retiring, leaving a vacancy for a new head of campus. Though Rudy hadn't yet built up much administrative experience, I thought it would be a good idea for him to apply. I could see him thriving in that role, and I knew his colleagues would, too.

But Rudy hesitated. Thinking solely of me, he saw the longer hours and countless after-school commitments that would likely come with the new position. He worried about the added weight I'd have to carry—managing everything at home alone: the kids, the cats, the house, and my real estate career.

Staying at home with kids was not something I fully embraced. We often joke about the reversed roles in our relationship—give Rudy an apron and me a tool belt. The thought of him being out of the house even more felt like uncharted territory for us, and he was reluctant to disrupt our balance. But I urged him, *"Get the job first, and then we'll have something more to discuss."*

Rudy applied, and although he wasn't offered the position, the experience opened another door, one he hadn't seen coming. He was encouraged to apply for a newly posted assistant principal position, and that opportunity became a pivotal stepping stone in his career. The hours were longer, the dynamic at home shifted, but as a family, we adapted. And like tossing a medicine ball back and forth in the gym, we took turns catching and carrying the weight.

One Step at a Time

Last year, while prepping for my third week in the *Goldman Sachs 10,000 Small Businesses Program,* I had to be talked off the ledge. I was so overwhelmed I considered quitting the program just as it was getting started. I hadn't realized how much work was involved when I committed to participating. I'd missed the second session due to a girls' trip planned before my acceptance into the program. I assumed catching up would be easy. Well, you know what they say about assuming—needless to say, I was wrong.

The sessions were intense—full days of learning, followed by assignments which required time, energy, and brainpower. It was just the beginning and it already felt like my brain would burst. To ensure I'd make it to the early Thursday morning class easier and on time, I planned to stay at a hotel in Long Island City where the sessions were being held. It was now 2:30PM on Wednesday, the night before class.

I had a million and one things to do—emails to respond to, homework to complete for the class, and I still had to pack. I had a growing sense of dread about driving in an unfamiliar area at night, as I was planning to meet up with Anthony, one of my new GS10kSB cohorts in Yonkers so we could drive into LIC together.

Then my phone buzzed. First, a message from Anthony:

"Hey, not feeling great. Might leave earlier to go to the hotel and take a nap."

Not what I wanted to hear. I was desperately counting on that ride.

Then, a text from my **10KSB group advisor**:

"Please complete your Competitive Mapping Tools ASAP. It's dragging your growth group's score down."

Ugh! That was it. The straw that broke the camel's back.

"I think I am going to stop here," I responded to my advisor. I was ready to quit the program. I immediately fired off a text to *Rudy*, *"I'm going to resign from Goldman. There's too much on my plate right now. I really just don't have the time."*

With Rudy in a meeting at work, I expected a short response—something supportive, like "I understand." But he fired back, *"I think that's a bad idea. Let's discuss before you make any decisions, please."*

My reply? A long-winded rant about how exhausted I was and how much I still had to do.

"One step at a time." He replied.

"I'll drive you tonight. And then we figure out the rest."

His response was simple. **Calm. Unshaken.**

That was all it took; the weight was lifted. Rudy has a way of seeing beyond my panic, grounding me before I spiral too far. And he was right—one step at a time. That was all I needed to focus on.

The Power of Partnership

That's what true partnership is. Sometimes, we have to be the voice of reason for each other. Experiences such as these have shaped how Rudy and I approach challenges together. We embrace each new obstacle side by side, climbing the ladder one step at a time. Instead of prematurely talking ourselves out of opportunities, we explore them fully before making a decision.

Our philosophy is simple: **pursue first, figure out the details later**. We don't let uncertainty hold us back from something that could change our lives for the better. And neither should you. Be sure you and your *iron love* openly communicate what you envision for your union. Remain receptive to weaving each other's philosophies into your shared life. It's not about being right, it's about discovering what's right together. Always lift each other up and encourage one another to reach for the stars… especially if you want to be amazed by the *bird's eye view*.

The beauty of love is that it doesn't just shine in moments of success and growth—it is tested, refined, and strengthened in times of uncertainty and hardship. We don't always know what life will throw our way, but when love is deeply rooted in mutual support and fully committed to, and incorporated into our lives, it becomes the anchor that steadies us through even the stormiest of times.

And sometimes, love is tested in ways we never could have imagined.

TRUSTING LOVE

SURRENDER

Surrender I fall back.
Lifeless. Motionless.
His hand under my head.
I extend my arms.
The water lifts me up.
It supports my shell.
My eyes are open.
Widely I see.
When I hold my breath.
My body rises.
He's the designee.
I let him lead.
Choosing my direction.
My legs awake.
Lightly move with grace.
I observe the clouds.
Above me they trail.
Never seen this way.

The most beautiful day.

He supports my soul.

It's ok to breathe.

I can surrender.

He's got my back.

My mind is clear.

My heart is full.

I surrender.

It's ok to be.

It's ok to be.

-Kenyatta Jones-Arietta

∽

By Oxford Languages' definition, trust is "a firm belief in the reliability, truth, ability, or strength of someone or something." In business, trust is essential. I trust that my team of real estate professionals will do everything in their power to negotiate the best terms for our clients' home purchases and sales transactions. But trust isn't just about high-stakes decisions, it also exists in the smallest, most predictable moments of daily life.

For example, I trust that when our four-year-old Great Dane Bruce hears or sees our neighbor's dog, Huck, he will immediately head to the nearest door, eager to be let outside to bark at him… incessantly. And when he trots back inside, proudly, as if he just did something wonderful, Bruce *will* proceed to his favorite spot on the sofa, right next to the picture window in the family room, to lounge in the sunlight. If he didn't follow this pattern, we would all wonder if he was sick. We trust him to do what we've always known him to do.

In a March 2024 interview with TIME magazine, trust thought leader Rachel Botsman, author of *Who Can You Trust?* states, "Trust is like energy—it doesn't get destroyed; it changes form. It's not a question of whether you trust; it's where you place your trust." After being burned by touching a hot pot, you *trust* that touching another pot, which has been boiling on a stove, will produce the same result. Therefore, you learn not to touch a hot pot with your bare hands. This doesn't mean you avoid the pot entirely—it simply means you know you should use an oven mitt for protection to avoid being burned next time.

I am reminded again of the saying "When someone shows you who they are, believe them." I'd been burned (figuratively) by almost every person I was intimately connected with and bearing witness to my mother's failed relationships didn't give me confidence that a happy, loving, committed relationship was achievable. Combine that limiting belief with the dark side of men I observed during my club days—one wouldn't blame me for being a forever skeptic. Yet even with what I witnessed and experienced, I never lost hope.

I was open to the idea of someday finding true love—allowing myself to fall back into someone's arms, feeling confident that they would catch me—but trust did not happen overnight. For Rudy and me, it took time to build the level of trust and vulnerability we share today. With my past relationship scars, it took a while to feel comfortable letting my guard down completely. It wasn't until around year thirteen that we truly reached the depth we share now. That's not to say our relationship wasn't trusting before—we had to make it that far—but like anything worth having, *deep trust* requires time, tests, growth, and effort.

Deep trust is a journey, not a destination. At every stage, you can discover new layers of intimacy and openness in your relationship. And if you think you've reached the pinnacle of connection, I'm here to gently challenge you. Love and trust can always grow deeper. There's always more to explore if both partners are willing to put in the work. Some couples may feel content with where they are, and that's okay if both parties are genuinely happy. But for Rudy and me, growth has always been the fuel that keeps us moving forward—individually, and as a couple; both in our personal and professional lives.

∽

Rudy and I met at Lace, a strip club in West Nyack, NY. Just like you can encounter the devil in a place of worship, you can also connect with good people in the most unlikely places. Rudy wasn't the only guy I'd ever dated from my club days, but he was the last. It wasn't love at first sight. It was work—I mean, I was literally working. Like Ani, the main character in Sean Baker's 2024 film *Anora*, I made my rounds in the club that evening, approaching Rudy just as I had many others before him. "Hi. Would you like a dance?" I asked him, smiling with a mouth full over pearly whites that glowed under the black lights. With a *"yes"* from his lips, I took him by the hand and escorted him up to the private room where he sat in a swivel barrel club chair, waiting for the next song to begin.

Watching Anora's opening scene was like stepping into a memory. The dim lights, flashing strobes, pulsating music—the unspoken transactions of attention and allure—it was all so familiar. While Ani's world extended beyond the stage into escorting, mine did not. I danced, I performed, I made money from the art of seduction—and that is where the similarities between the movie and my life ended.

The length of a table dance was determined by the length of the song played—a single dance lasted for about three to four minutes. And depending on the energy of the customer, that could feel like an eternity. In between dances and mingling with would-be patrons, as performers, we were required to do sets on either the main or bar stage. A set consisted of three dances. The first was performed to one song in full costume, which for me was typically some short, sexy dress, exposing my long lean legs, in a light color that popped against my chocolate brown skin.

I was partial to wearing white, as it glowed under the black lights, making it easy to find me from across the dark, often crowded club. Tops were dropped with song two and by number three, I stripped down to my g-string, heels, and a garter—a necessary accessory for collecting tips. I performed one single dance for Rudy that first night. He was respectful, but there were clear indicators that he enjoyed the performance. We didn't see each other again until about three to four weeks later. We met just before spring break, days before Tiera and I headed to Puerto Rico for a little mommy/daughter getaway. The next time Rudy and I encountered one another, we talked a bit before my performance.

The initial conversation consisted of basic "getting to know you" chit-chatter, which is typically used to solicit more dances. There was definite chemistry between us. It wasn't long before Rudy became my ride back to Queens from West Nyack after my shifts, which was around two or four o'clock in the morning. We listened to music and conversed as he sifted through traffic, navigating the Van Wyck. We talked about everything—music, movies, food, architecture—you name it, we probably discussed it.

It wasn't an immediate physical relationship, though it wasn't long before we were savoring the additional benefits of our budding friendship. I enjoyed our time together; I just couldn't see "us" long term. As shared previously, with what I'd seen from the likes of men, I wasn't sure I could see myself with anyone for too long. My suitors were either smothering, fleeting, or left me feeling insecure.

When Rudy and I first started talking, I introduced myself as an *independent 90s woman*. I didn't need a man; I could take care of myself. I can now see how living that mantra was like a curse. I thought I had to *present* myself as completely self-sufficient, not needing help from anyone, oblivious to the fact that in taking that stance, I was giving off vibes that a man was not needed.

This idea of independence left no room for a man to be a part of the equation. No, I did not *need* a man, but I did *want* a life partner. And I can honestly say I would not be where I am today without Rudy's unwavering love and support.

I encountered many types of beings in the club—the work buddies stopping in for a brew, the curious college kids, the mobster wannabees, the happily married, the hopeful hornies, the knights in shining armor, and even the occasional celebrity. I've entertained them all. The true colors some of them revealed—especially when alcohol was involved—made it astonishing that I ever grew to trust humans born with penises ever again.

Working in the club was, in many ways, like working almost anywhere that requires engaging with customers (except the customer wasn't always right). Most patrons were there simply to have a good time. But you could always count on one to try to take things too far. Every once in a while, someone would become downright sloppy drunk and belligerent—those childish characters I could do without.

Amid all the chaotic craziness I faced at work, Rudy became my safe haven. With him, I began to feel like I didn't need to be guarded. I could be my authentic, intensely energetic, creative, and sometimes spacey self. That honesty opened the door to the beginning of trust between the two of us.

Strip clubs were the first real club scene I'd ever been introduced to, and over time, they'd become like a second home to me. Later I found they weren't much different than any other nightclub or lounge, except if you worked there, you were allowed to be a little more… free.

During the beginning of our relationship Rudy and I would occasionally go to Lace to hang out when I wasn't working—sometimes just the two of us, other times with friends—blending into the atmosphere that had been central to my life. As time passed and our lives evolved, our visits became less frequent.

Fast-forward five years into our marriage—roughly two years after the birth of our first beautiful baby boy. I was no longer working in the club, but during that time, I stumbled upon something that made me question everything.

The Universe is always sending us signs— but when we're not ready for the lesson, we unconsciously choose to ignore them.

One day, while emptying Rudy's jacket pockets before dropping his clothes off at the dry cleaners, I found a receipt from a strip club. Judging by the amount on the bill, it must have been a pretty fun night—but one I wasn't a part of. In fact, I didn't recall getting an invite. *How dare he!* I confronted him with my findings, and to his credit, he didn't try to cover it up or pretend it didn't happen. He admitted he had gone without me and had engaged one of the entertainers.

"And the truth shall set you free," they say, but in that moment, the truth only set me off. Though I was comfortable being in the club environment with him, I was not okay with him going without me, especially without telling me. I was extremely hurt, disappointed, and felt betrayed. It felt like a violation of our fragile trust.

Remember earlier when I said Rudy and I don't argue? Well, before I could process this incident and approach the situation like a rational human being—before I could set my ego and emotions aside—our initial communication? That, my friend, was indeed an argument.

Like rubbing a magic lamp, the discovery unleashed all of the negative thoughts and feelings I had bottled up inside about men over the years—what I experienced in my own relationships, what I witnessed in the clubs, all of it!

"I guess this is what you men do!" I ranted, pacing between the dining room and living room, throwing myself into chores.

"You get us to fall in love with you, then you marry us..." I aggressively gathered laundry from around the house, tossing it into the basket with the force of a punch.

"You get us pregnant, and then you go off and do whatever the fuck you think you want to do!"

I marched into the kitchen, slamming pots onto the counter and in the sink. "Well, I'm not going to stay here for that!"

I turned to Rudy—my glare sharp enough to cut glass. "I'd rather be by myself than tolerate being disrespected."

I was beyond pissed. But in the same breath, I found myself wondering, *Is this my fault*? I wasn't in the shape I was when we met, having just had a baby. I was pouring so much of my attention into our little one—was I neglecting Rudy? Was I not giving him the attention he needed?

Then, like a bolt of lightning, another thought struck me:

That is bullshit! <u>THIS</u> is supposed to be a team effort.

We're in this together. Whether I gained two hundred pounds or not, he was supposed to support me—workout with me, go for walks with me while we strolled the baby, or how about even watch the baby so I could hit the gym myself? Because *that's* what we committed to.

After I calmed down and Rudy no longer had to fear for his life, we were able to fully communicate with one another. There were moments where I lost my cool while he was recounting the details of his one-man adventure. I remember sitting on the chaise of our sectional while he sat in the corner of the sofa, appearing remorseful yet cautious.

At one point, I got so angry just thinking about it that I *may have* thrown a pillow at him. No, I don't condone violence. And I was wrong—no matter how justified my anger felt at the time. But back then, I hadn't

Iron Love | 107

yet matured to where I am today, and, well, the pillow was launched. Rudy sat uneasily, like a little boy who knew he'd done something he shouldn't have, bracing for the consequences.

I leaned on my girlfriends for support, leaving Rudy home with the baby so I could let off some steam. I wanted him to feel what it was like to be stuck in the house with the little one all day, isolated from the world while I was out having a great time without him. The act itself didn't solve anything, but it was good to get out with my girls again.

At the end of the day, he just went to a strip club—something we did together on many occasions. He had a few drinks and a few dances. We hadn't yet discussed him going without me, and whether or not I would be cool with that. With the bond we built up to that point, the offense, in my opinion, wasn't worth throwing in the towel over.

I also recognize the level of maturity Rudy showed. He could have been upset with me for going out. Two wrongs don't make a right, but he allowed me the time and space to burn off steam without internalizing it as a personal attack. Talk about keeping ego in check. Rudy's understanding and patience allowed things to simmer down and rationalization to take hold.

No one is perfect. We are all human, all here learning. But after this incident, we both knew what was ok and what wouldn't fly (pillows included). We discussed it, we came to a resolution, and we moved on with our lives. It took a while to fully trust again that if he didn't come straight home, he wasn't at the club without me. I went through a period of looking for signs of "misconduct" where they didn't exist.

Sometimes, if you're not in a place of trust in your relationship, you might start looking for signs that don't exist and inadvertently manifest the very thing you fear. Be careful with projecting. We humans have incredibly powerful minds, and our thoughts can create realities. Thankfully, with communication, consistency and time, all was right in the world between us again. That is, until the next season of growing pains, which came about nine years later.

2013 was a very interesting year for us, to say the least. Bodybuilding had become a big part of our lives, and I'd just completed my first year competing as a figure pro. Rudy and I had been competing in bodybuilding non-stop for over three years—we went from one competition prep to the next.

Prepping for competitions was much like planning for a wedding or any other major event—you searched for the perfect bikini or posing trunks. And if your competition attire wasn't prêt-à-porter (ready to wear) you selected a suit designer, fabric color and print, as well as the color bling for your suit.

So many decisions to make: hairstyle, nail color, nail design and shape, spray tanner, makeup palette, and whether you're doing your makeup yourself or hiring a makeup artist. For shoes, to give the illusion of being barefoot, most female competitors (figure and bikini) wore see-through plastic slippers in varying heel heights and styles, but bodybuilders traditionally perform barefoot. Last, but not least, one of, if not the most important decision of all…

Where you're going to go for your cheat meal after the night show.

It was quite the production, not to mention the countless days of strength training and cardio in between work and family time. Towards the end of my final competition season, I was doing 2 workouts a day, 6-7 days a week. It was mentally and physically exhausting. I began to feel a little like, o*kay, that was fun. What's next?*

Since I was resigned to the fact that I wasn't going to compete again any time soon, I had to find something to replace the time I spent food-prepping and training. And then it hit me—*a healthy fast-food restaurant!* I couldn't think of a better project to sink my teeth into.

With a fitting name in mind, I created a protein-based menu featuring delicious, original culinary creations perfect for health-conscious consumers. In addition, the eatery would serve breakfast, showcasing my signature *Clean Girl, Dirty Girl* pancakes. The name came from all the *clean* (high protein, low fat, low sugar) recipes I created from traditionally *dirty* (sugar and/or fat-filled) dishes. I turned all of my favorite cake flavors into stackable, protein-rich hotcakes. If you want to try a few of my recipes, remnants can be found in cyberspace at kenyattafit.blogspot.com. Carrot cake, German Chocolate cake, lemon cake, you name it, I had a pancake or no-bake protein bar to match it, yet more research and planning were needed to ensure the venture's success.

As if navigating my transition from competing to entrepreneurship wasn't mentally taxing enough, Rudy and I received some life altering news. We were going to be grandparents.

Yep! Grandparents!!! I was just 41 and Rudy, 38—I was in the best shape of my life. Our boys were only seven and ten. I was actively selling real estate in Rockland and Orange Counties while still managing East Coast events for *Power Crunch*. In fact, I was scheduled to manage a team for the protein company at The *New Life Expo* in Manhattan when the *baby bomb* was dropped. It was A LOT to process.

Tiera was only 24, just out of college and hadn't yet begun a career. She wasn't married, nor in a serious relationship with her baby daddy. And me? ***I was too young to be somebody's grandma.*** My mind raced as I drove down the West Side Highway, en route to the New York Hotel, where the expo was being held. I thought about my life—where it was headed and what this new role meant. Becoming a grandparent was huge! Did this mean I was no longer young? But I was still too young to be old.

There were so many things I still wanted to do and experience. At that moment in our lives, with the kids being so young and our work commitments piling up, Rudy and I started to feel more like business partners than the hot, steamy couple we were when we first connected. Somewhere along the way, we stopped being Kenyatta and Rudy and had predominantly become Mom and Dad. And soon we would be Nana and Pop-Pop.

Wait. What?!

I looked out at the Hudson River, watching the sun's reflection shimmer over the waves and skyscrapers as I passed by. The wind caressed my hair as it whispered, "*Everything is going to be okay.*" I tried to distract myself by focusing on something less intense.

I had plans to meet up with a few old friends, which was customary. When I travel, I make it a point to connect with people I know in the area. It's part of the experience. Since I mostly traveled alone, the meetups helped to pass the time while strengthening old connections. *Two birds. One stone.*

That particular weekend, I had plans to meet up with two male friends, Matteo and Jamal, who I hadn't seen in quite some time. Now before you start thinking *"How could I?"* Don't worry, Rudy knew about them. One of the many reasons we work is that he's neither possessive nor insecure.

Matteo was one of the last guys I dated before Rudy and I met. As mentioned earlier, he was the one who, thirteen years prior, pointed out that he thought Rudy was good for me. We met up for dinner that first night before the expo began. Afterward, I met up with Jamal for cocktails.

Jamal wasn't an ex. We knew each other from the nightclub scene (**not** the strip club). He was a great dancer, among other things—all very casual. After drinks, I dropped Jamal off at a subway station before heading to the hotel to park my car. Just before opening the door to get out, he looked me in my eyes and leaned in to kiss me goodbye.

That kiss—it was as if we were briefly transported back to the *good ole days*, when we were all so young and carefree (**can't believe I'm calling the 90s the good ole days**). And then, back to reality. Jamal exited the car, flashing his pearly whites, a striking contrast against his caramel-colored skin, before disappearing into the night.

The weekend was transformative. The expo was filled with fascinating vendors and spiritual healers. I received my first (and only) energy adjustment by a *Quantum healer* whose booth happened to be right next to ours.

There are no coincidences.

I received readings from two different psychics, along with a sage cleaning and massage from one of the most beautiful human beings with the most amazing healing energy. Though some of what I experienced seemed to be a bit *woo-woo* or far out, I returned home with a renewed sense of clarity—not just about Tiera's pregnancy, but also about my own path. It was then I decided to put a pin in the restaurant idea and create my own real estate brokerage instead.

I felt completely confident in the new direction of my life, at least as far as business was concerned. I had already incorporated the name, **R2M Realty, Inc.,** though initially, it was only for tax purposes. After working under three different franchises, I knew what I liked (and what I didn't) about each of them.

By creating my own brokerage, I could build operations around what I believed worked best, eliminating the need for permissions from anyone else. Having already achieved my associate broker's license, getting started was as easy as a few clicks on the New York Department of State website. Opening a restaurant, on the other hand, would have required significantly more time and energy to get it off the ground. It all made sense. It was as if the weekend cleared my head so that I was able to *see*, removing the bulk of uncertainty to reveal a lean, focused path.

But my wonderful husband, the man with whom I share a very deep and soulful connection, sensed something was off when I walked through the door. Remember, the Universe gives us signs—all of us, **including** my Rudy.

We either see or feel something, and it's just a matter of whether we choose to tap into that feeling and press on it or make a conscious decision to let it go. Of course, there are times when a partner may be projecting their own sins, insecurities, or doubt, but this was not one of them. Rudy didn't initially share what he was feeling. He held on to it until an incident one morning shortly after my return.

We were standing in the middle of our kitchen. I don't remember what we were talking about, but I asked Rudy to retrieve his aunt's phone number from the contacts. As he went to unlock my phone, there was a *ping*—followed by a moment of silence.

"Kenyatta."

I knew something was wrong when he said my name. He usually calls me "*Sweet Lover*" or "*Angel of Mercy*"..

"*I wasn't trying to look at your messages or anything—but I saw this.*"

Rudy's eyes met mine. He looked as though someone had just punched him in the gut as he turned the screen toward me, exposing an image of Matteo's scantily clad body in boxers.

Rudy stood there, stunned, needing an explanation.

(Way to go Matteo!)

If you were friends with Rudy and I (or any other bodybuilder, for that matter) during competition days , you've probably received at least one progress pic—in bikini, boxers, or briefs—documenting an athlete's unbelievable transformation. It's actually quite impressive.

When I competed, I shared photos with anyone (male or female) remotely interested in seeing my progress. Even now, if you're curious, you need look no further than Facebook or Google to find snapshots from the Arietta bodybuilding era. There are still quite a few out there. Matteo was just showing off his progress—nothing more, nothing less. Mortified by how it must have looked to Rudy, I blurted out, *"Oh gosh! It's not what you think!"* My face turned beet red with embarrassment. *"It's totally not what you think."*

I tried reassuring Rudy there was nothing between Matteo and me. I even called Matteo, who immediately confirmed that Rudy's suspicions were off. Matteo apologized for causing such an upset. But Rudy couldn't seem to shake it off. Something in his *core* just didn't sit right. Yes, I married a man who is as intuitive as I am. (That wasn't on my manifestation list, by the way, but it's definitely a bonus.)

After a day or so, Rudy finally opened up, telling me, *"I know you both said there is nothing, but I'm still not settled."* In the back of his mind, Rudy felt that Matteo saw me as *the one who got away*. While he was okay with our friendship, he also believed Matteo would take an *opportunity* if he were ever given one.

It had to be the kiss, I thought. *Rudy must be feeling something from the kiss with Jamal.* To me, the kiss meant so little that I hadn't given it a second thought—I had already moved on. But I knew I had to come clean.

"Rudy," I said, turning to look him in his eyes. *"It's the right feeling, but the wrong person."*

As I shared earlier, Jamal and I had never dated. We shared a few steps on the dance floor and a few convenient romps in the sack, but nothing formal or exclusive. Jamal was just a charming party promoter with a hypnotic, boyish smile and crazy, *you-just-want-to-get-your-hands-wrapped-up-in-it* hair. He had a cool vibe, great moves, and was fun to hang with.

The kiss Jamal and I shared before he got out of the car? It was intimate. Oh yeah—it was a nice, sloppy one. (I cover my face from embarrassment) but that's all it was. Trust me, I have no reason to start fabricating now. I knew it wasn't the "*appropriate*" thing to do, but it was done.

Rudy—the man that knows me about as well as I know myself—was relieved that his Spidey-senses were on point. But he was disappointed and hurt. I would have been too. We sought counseling after the incident, and what came out of it wasn't what you might expect.

"It's not the kiss that bothers me; it's the fact that you kept it from me."

Much like the strip club incident, it wasn't the act itself—it was the lack of communication that created the disconnect and shook our foundation of trust. In Rudy's eyes, by not sharing the incident with him, I had created an intimate connection—a secret—with Jamal. And there should never be anyone outside of your union who knows more about you than your *iron love*. By not telling Rudy about the moment I shared with Jamal, I had unintentionally given Jamal—a character making a guest appearance in *The Rudy and Kenyatta Show*—a connection to me that should have been reserved for the co-star of your life's production, and that, right there, was the part Rudy struggled to accept.

Now before you start slipping in our DMs—no, we don't have an open relationship where we just *communicate* what we're doing or have done. **It's not that type of party**. But we both rest assured knowing there are no secrets between us. As we worked to rebuild trust and strengthen our communication, I opened up about how I was feeling in our relationship—my desire to bring more of "*us*" back into our marriage. Just because we were parents (and soon to be grandparents) didn't mean we should lose who we were as a couple.

We were still just beginning and personally, I'm not trying to *be old*. There's still so much I want to do this lifetime (individually and as a unit). I also didn't want to be the only one to come up with ideas of things to do together. I shared with Rudy my desire for a *dance partner*. He heard me, and his actions proved it.

Rudy started sending me ideas of things we could do together, or even planning them himself without me having to make a single decision. Between running a household and a business, there are times I just don't want to think about one more thing. Then there are moments when I flip that, reminding myself that Rudy's position mirrors mine. Sometimes he doesn't want to think either, and I honor that. It's the give and take. The balance. A dance.

∽

The journey of life is never without lessons. What fun would living be without the knowledge we gain and the emotions we experience along the way? These teachings enlighten us, shape us, and push us forward.

Ultimately, what Rudy and I learned through the experiences is that **communication *is* truly the key**—and that strengthening a relationship requires active and conscious effort every single day. Loving relationships require that you "do" and not just "be," and trust is paramount for iron love to grow and flourish.

Like a tango, which demands a strong connection between partners, there are moments when one person takes the lead. At other times, the tempo shifts, requiring the other partner to trust and follow, relying on their counterpart's intricate footwork and sharp moves to execute the dance seamlessly.

Both participants must be willing and able to relinquish control at times, letting their partner lead, trusting they will guide them along the right path.

But what happens when trusting your partner leads you down the wrong path?

⁂

A dear friend of mine, Simone, recently confided in me that her husband of 23 years, the father of her children, the man she trusted to handle the family finances, had squandered their life savings trying to rescue his failing business. The fallout left them with no choice but to sell off all of their assets just to stop the bleeding.

Now, after more than two decades as a stay-at-home mom, Simone has returned to the workplace, just when she should be preparing for retirement. It was a harsh reality, one that took time to comprehend.

She shared with me that there were signs long before things reached this breaking point, which is why it's so important to pay attention to the signals you receive instead of sweeping them under the rug. Addressing disconnects as they arise, pinpointing the issues, understanding their impact, and working together to resolve them is the only way to move forward.

Broken trust isn't just about infidelity or financial deceit. It's in the everyday assurances—you *trust* that when your partner says they're going to work, that's where they're going. You trust that when they say the bills are paid, the money is in the bank, or the savings are secure, they've handled it.

But when trust is breached, it can shake the very core of your relationship. If something feels off—if you've never doubted before but suddenly notice something that gives you pause—**trust your instincts**. Communicate your concerns. Burying your head in the sand for too long can lead to irreversible damage. Ignoring the warning signs is like pushing through bad form while weight training—eventually something's going to break or strain.

Regaining trust requires effort. If the damage runs deep, rebuilding it may require a substantial amount of work, both, individually and as a couple to get back to the level of vulnerability you once shared. Sometimes, one or both partners may lack the energy or will to continue on the path together, ultimately deciding to part ways and move forward separately.

༄

How do you get back to trusting love?

Both you and your partner must actively work at rebuilding trust. Remember earlier when I shared that loving relationships require you to *do* and not just to *be*? **Doing** begins with confronting the situation head-on, understanding when the trust was broken and identifying how the disconnect grew. Together, you must develop solutions to prevent it from happening again.

Share your feelings with your partner and allow them to share theirs without becoming defensive. It can be painful and uncomfortable, but **iron love is worth a weighted walk through the mud uphill.**

Avoid approaching the situation from a place of anger. It's difficult to communicate effectively, think clearly, or process emotions when your blood is boiling. Wait until you are both calm before initiating reconciliation. Once you've discussed the issue and agreed on viable solutions, **move forward.** Picking at a scab before the wound has completely healed only prolongs the process and may cause your partner to become defensive and shut down.

If the challenge feels too overwhelming to handle on your own, consider seeking help from a relationship specialist or marriage counselor. Don't just go with the one your girlfriend Suzy recommended—interview potential counselors to find someone who **you both trust.** Breakdowns with counseling often occur when one partner feels the therapist is taking sides. Even if that's not the case, if one person feels unheard or misunderstood, they may withdraw. If you choose to work through the challenges, both partners must **fully commit** to reconnecting and giving it their all.

In some cases, the relationship may not survive. You may choose to walk down a different path, a new path, alone. And that's okay. It's your life. Your journey. Life is too short and unpredictable to spend it being perpetually unhappy. But if your bond is strong, if it's truly meant to be, after time spent healing and growing as individuals, you may choose each other again, choosing to build an Iron Love.

꿏

Let's go back to our friends Lonnie and Lisa from Rockland. Owners of the popular bar restaurant in Clarkstown, they were married and lived together for 14 years before deciding to call it quits.

Lisa *didn't trust* Lonnie, and from what they shared when I sat down with them, Lonnie had definitely given Lisa reasons not to. Lonnie wanted to have his cake and eat it too. He wanted to be able to flirt and *hangout* with other women and still have Lisa at home. Lisa wasn't going to stand for it and so they decided to go their separate ways.

During their separation, they co-parented their children and continued running the restaurant together. Eventually, Lisa left the business and opened her own med spa, which gave her a newfound sense of independence and confidence. Running her own business left her with no time to worry about Lonnie's every move.

When they were together before their divorce, they were husband and wife raising a traditional Italian family with traditional family values. But they weren't *friends*. During their time apart, they learned to connect as friends—and in doing so, they discovered a balance between their relationship, parenting, and work that deepened their love fostered with open communication and trust.

Even while separated, they continued taking family vacations together, staying in separate rooms and spending time together only with their kids. Lonnie continued to go over to Lisa's house for dinner and spend time with the boys, but he never stayed over. "He had his own apartment. And if he [Lonnie] ever needed anything…" Lisa paused, emotional, as she reflected on that time in their lives to me, implying that she would always be there for Lonnie. "I always loved him."

Lisa imitated how Lonnie would play around with her in a loving way after they had time to heal and grow as individuals. When I asked the couple what they learned during their separation and divorce. Lisa began, "My life lessons were… you have to appreciate *your partner* and you have to work at the relationship and when you love somebody, you have to…" Lisa took a deep breath trying to keep her composure. She was visibly holding back tears. "Commit", Lonnie finished Lisa's sentence, placing his hand on her arm to console her. I saw the gentle gesture as his way of saying, *"I'm here my love."*

"Here's what I learned." Lonnie leaned in. "I really was alone for six and a half years. I examined myself and I realized I was a selfish person. You know, you have to *give*," he emphasized. "I had these old-fashioned standards…

"Well, it should be like this.

This is how it was."

I realized I was selfish. I wasn't *giving*… and I realized I really loved her." Lonnie looked Lisa in the eyes. "I missed her terribly."

Lisa gazed at Lonnie and smiled as he continued. "And I learned that you really have to make a commitment to work on the relationship." Lonnie again looked over at Lisa with a twinkle in his eye. "I don't know. I guess, right?"

"Yeah," Lisa continued. "He is actually better at communicating now", implying that Lonnie *committed* to working on openly expressing himself over time. "Communication. Yes," Lonnie agrees.

I later learned that COVID may have been the reconnector. Living through the pandemic independently made Lisa and Lonnie realize how much they still really loved each other. Lonnie contracted the virus in March of 2020. He was down for 13 days with high fever. Lisa took care of him, dropping off food and supplies at his doorstep as needed. From what they shared, the way Lisa cared for Lonnie while he was battling the virus was a far cry from the emotion and attention she showed the man she was dating during their separation, who at one point, believed he was having a heart attack.

On the flip side, Lonnie was constantly at odds with his then girlfriend, who grew frustrated every time he would refer to Lisa as his wife. It rolled off of his tongue naturally as if it were meant to be. Actions speak volumes. No one ever really stood a chance against Lonnie and Lisa's Iron Love.

They decided to get back together in June of 2020 and planned a family vacation in the Bahamas that November, which coincidentally, would have been their original 20th wedding anniversary. "Twenty minus six and a half." Lisa chimed in, not counting the time they were apart. They were discussing the plans for their upcoming getaway when Lisa jokingly commented that they should renew their vows.

Before you knew it, "Lonnie planned the whole event." Lisa recounts. "He said, 'I've got a guy... we're going to get married on the beach... This day, this time...'"

Lonnie chimed in, "photographer and all!"

"The old Lonnie would have never done anything like that. He is just different now—[and] I'm the happiest I've ever been." Lisa remarked.

Not only had Lonne changed, so had Lisa. It was like a domino effect: Lonnie's commitment to growth, being more attentive, communicating openly, and actively participating in their relationship, rather than just holding the title of husband, created a sense of comfort and trust for Lisa. Because of that newfound trust, Lisa no longer felt the need to question him. Her absence of nagging and questioning, allowed him to feel more at ease, which in turn, deepened his desire to do more.

And that, my friend, is what trust is all about. Pour into me and I will pour into you. Through constant reassurance and mutual reciprocation, we begin to let our guards down—to be vulnerable, knowing—just knowing that our Iron Love is real and present. Because what's communicated is honest and true, and reinforced by persistent, consistent action. Without commitment and trust as the foundation, anything built above it can very easily be shaken... or fall.

SUPPORTING LOVE

Supporting love goes beyond bolstering each other's professional, spiritual and physical desires, especially when you choose to have children and build a family unit. As parents there are moments when you are tested and pushed to unimaginable limits. Standing by each other is paramount—and in those trying times, being open to receiving the support from others can make all the difference. Your lives may even depend on it.

Rudy and I faced one of our greatest challenges of our lives when our daughter was 26. The memories of that time are etched so deeply in my soul it still gives me chills. Tiera had been prescribed an antidepressant known to cause numbness in some users. After months of complaining about what we believed was unrelated acute back pain likely stemming from her Tae Kwon Do practice, she began experiencing numbness in her toes.

Knowing the correlation between the medication and numbness, I suggested she stop taking the prescription to see if the symptom would subside. In the meantime, Tiera scheduled an MRI (magnetic resonance imaging) to see what was going on with her back. After multiple visits to the chiropractor, it just didn't seem to be improving.

Rudy and I were sitting in the family room by the fireplace when Tiera received the call. She walked into the room, "So, I'm on the phone with my doctor. Based on the MRI results, she thinks this could be an infection." Tiera paused. "Or cancer." She rolled her eyes, annoyed by the notion, as if to say, *There is no way this can really be cancer*". She continued. "The doctor wants to have me admitted so they can run more tests."

Rudy and I looked up at her, then at each other. *Wait. What?!*

There has to be some mistake, I thought. From that moment, everything began to move at lightning speed—it all felt surreal.

Less than two days later, Tiera was admitted to *Good Samaritan Hospital* in Suffern, NY. A contrast MRI performed that day revealed a mass on her spine, left glute, and the left side of her pelvis. The following day, a biopsy was conducted, leading doctors to believe that our daughter had a rare cancer and would need to be referred to a specialist.

How could this be possible? How does a 26-year-old get cancer? I was in shock. It was a lot to process in such a short period of time.

Meanwhile, Rudy and I still had work, our boys, who were 9 and 12 at the time and in the absence of Tiera, our two-year-old granddaughter, Raevyn to care for in between running back and forth to the hospital. We tackled the mission like the true team we are, but when I walked through the door of our home at night, my energy dropped like a weighted garment slipping from my shoulders onto the floor—I had nothing left to give.

When they say, "*It takes a village*"... I don't know how we would have survived that time without ours. Our friend Patricia babysat our little Rae of sunshine before she went to stay with our friends, Damien, and Clarissa, who had littles around her age. Our neighbor Beverly came to the house in the mornings to make breakfast and get the boys off to school that first week. Then our son Sean went to stay with his friend Dylan and his family, while our cousins Debbie and Dennis looked after not-so-little Rudy. And my girlfriend, Nicole—the freaking rockstar, she is—stayed with our baby girl in the hospital when we couldn't be by her side.

Each new day brought with it a new challenge to contend with. "*Why us?!*" I found myself screaming at the top of my lungs in my moments alone. At the same time, channeling the thought that *everything happens for a reason,* wondering **what's the lesson we're supposed to learn from this**? Even now, tears well up as I write, remembering that time... and then came the morning it all really started to settle in. The house was so quiet and still, almost lifeless aside from the sounds of our breathing.

The morning rays warmed my face. I whispered, "I don't want to get up," curled up in bed next to Rudy, not ready to face the reality of the new day. He pulled me closer. Tears began to stream from the corners of my eyes, across the bridge of my nose, landing on my pillow. I could hear Rudy sniffling. The pain we felt lay quietly tucked between the two of us.

As parents, we're supposed to be able to support our children—to kiss their booboos away and make everything better. Though we could advocate for Tiera's care, we had no control over what she was experiencing now, and we couldn't just *will* it away.

Then reality hit—why *not* us? I began to think. *What made us special or exempt from any of life's curveballs?*

No matter what happened, we knew we would have to **live** through it. The kids needed us to keep getting up every morning. *We* needed *us* to keep getting up every morning. Like the last rep before your arms give out from exhaustion during pushups, we had to work through the pain, finding strength in each other, trusting that on the other side of it all, we would all be better and wiser having gone through the experience together. From the moment Tiera was admitted to the hospital, I began pleading on my Facebook page:

Jan. 25, 2016- Asking for positivity and prayers for my girl, Tiera R. Focusing on a healing of her spine. An MRI done Friday showed a mass pinching her nerves causing her numbness in the lower parts of her body. Her doctor is running tests and monitoring the pain. We should know in a few days exactly what's what. Thank you in advance for your positive energy and support.

My time on this planet has shown me again and again that the collective energies of many can move mountains. We needed all of the positive energy we could get to help heal our girl. Like a rainbow appearing after a storm, it was as though accepting our situation and appealing to our loved ones began to shift the tides.

That morning, Rudy kissed me on the head, pulled back the covers and got up to start the day. I remained tucked in, reaching over to grab my mobile from the nightstand. I opened Facebook to find a message from one of our acquaintances, Dave Panzerella:

Hi Kenyatta. I have been reading your posts and am praying for the best for your daughter. As I may have mentioned I work in the Oncology research field and a really good friend of mine is the Chairman of Hematology and

Oncology at Columbia. I am praying your daughter does not need an introduction to him but if she does, please let me know as they use an awesome approach where they do a complete genomic sequence of the tumor and use that info to treat the patient. Once again, I am praying for the best but when I read "mass" and "spine" it is always of concern. God Bless. Dave

That motivated me to sit up and plant my feet on the floor. I stretched. "We'll get through this together," Rudy whispered. He kissed me again as he headed out the door. "I love you." Minutes later, I received yet another message. This time from Sean Keenan, a prominent builder in our community:

I'm sorry 2 c your daughter has some health issue. It appears 2 b something with her spine from your post. I have had back surgery. I had Dr Roger Hartle. He is the head of the spine institute @ Weil Cornell in Columbia Presbyterian hospital. Might be worth a look, all he does is spinal. Best of luck.

I headed to the kitchen to call Sean for more information. As I poured my first cup of coffee, my mobile rang. It was Dr. Jeffrey Oppenheim, one of the neurosurgeons at Good Sam.

"If we don't remove the mass from your daughter's spine, she may have irreversible nerve damage. I have time to operate later this morning."

Talk about *divine timing*—the conversation with Sean prepped me for the call with Dr. Oppenheim. Our prayers were being answered. I called Rudy to bring him up to speed. We planned to meet at the hospital before Tiera's surgery. Once we arrived, we joined our friend Nicole in the lounge, awaiting an update after the procedure. Still in scrubs, Dr. Oppenheim eventually came in to personally deliver the news. We rose to our feet, as he walked in, removing his surgical mask.

"We were able to successfully remove the mass from Tiera's spine. It came off very easily. We're going to test the tissue and should have results in a day or so. She did good." He smiled, looking each of us in the eyes. "She should be up and running in no time," he offered.

We all thanked Dr. Oppenheim, smiled, and exhaled in relief. The news offered a sense of calm, though we knew we weren't completely out of the woods. This battle was won, but the war wasn't over.

With the tissue removed from her spine, the team at Good Sam was able to properly diagnose her condition: A diffused large B Cell Lymphoma; a highly aggressive, yet very treatable cancer most common in Asian and Caucasian men, ages 60 and up. Our Tiera fit neither description, but a warrior she was. And as a family, we were poised to fight for her life together.

In an attempt to restore our family unit, we brought the kids back home, including Tiera. She began chemotherapy at Columbia Medical Doctors in Manhattan within days of the initial spine surgery. To commemorate the beginning of Tiera's treatment, we decided to take the family out for a special night—dinner at Carmine's in Times Square, followed by *The Lion King on Broadway*. "Time to go!", Rudy called for the crew. We employed a sitter to stay home with Rae.

The boys came downstairs dressed in black denim jeans and long-sleeved button-downs—Sean's all black and little Rudy's black and white plaid. Tiera made her way down with a fresh buzz cut that accentuated her face, having just chopped off her locks in preparation for chemo. She wore a deep burgundy velvet dress and a hopeful smile. She looked beautiful.

Dinner was great. It was wonderful to have the family all together again and to see their cheerful faces. We captured a single photo of us before we headed to the theatre. We were all excited to see the show. As we sat in our theatre seats and *The Circle of Life* scene was played out, I was moved to tears.

That's really what it was, wasn't it? The circle of our life—expression of unity and the unbreakable bonds of love and legacy. We showed up for our baby girl, by her side in lockstep. Every appointment, every prayer, every tear shed. It was about rising together with love, loyalty and unwavering commitment to support our child while also supporting each other and being lifted by our loving community.

It is often said that what you concentrate on grows. We were done with giving energy to fear, anger, and sadness. We were open to more love, positivity, and joy. Balancing it all was by far one of the **greatest obstacles we've faced**—as parents, as a couple, and as a family. My and Rudy's communication game became even tighter, as we managed our professional obligations and juggled the kids' schedules. We continued supporting each other, yet embraced the love, kindness, and generosity from others around us.

In the midst of it all, we made it a point to prioritize time with one another whenever we could—whether it was for a walk in the woods, a quick massage, dinner out (just the two of us), it didn't matter. No, we didn't feel guilty about it—the only way we could be our best selves for our family was to continue to take care of and harness our own energy. This left us whole and capable of being whole and capable for everyone else. My biggest takeaways from that time in our lives:

- **It's important to find and/or create moments of joy during adversity that you all can feel and benefit from as a family.**
- **It's okay to continue to take care of yourself and your partner without feelings of guilt.** *You can't fill a cup from an empty well.* **You have to take care of yourself in order to be able to take care of anyone else.**
- **Tap into others for additional support when you're both being challenged. Don't be afraid to communicate that need. You never know who has resources that can help.**
- **Look for the lessons in all things. Remember, our reason for being is to learn and experience love and life.**

This chapter in our lives really showed Rudy and I that together we can get through almost anything. Now, when we face difficult moments in our lives, we reflect on the challenges we've championed together—it reminds us just how strong we are.

2016—that became the year our daughter battled cancer and won. While Tiera endured the pain of multiple surgeries, treatments, tests and giving what she could energetically to Raevyn, she wrote her first book, *Awakening: Bloodline Book One*. She also founded her publishing company, *Eula Rae Publishing*—the publisher of *Iron Love*.

As a family and as a community, we all focused on her healing, doing #26forTiera (26 pushups a day in honor of her age at the time of this journey)—controlling only the things we could. And getting up every day no matter how difficult it was. I had already navigated a lifetime of challenges before this chapter in our lives. And though it was severely heartbreaking to go through, this experience ultimately brought us closer as a family.

For every prayer, push-up, call, meal, babysitting shift, or positive thought sent our way—thank you from the bottom of my heart.

∽

A Love That Stood the Test of Time

Tiera's cancer scare wasn't the *first time* Rudy supported me through a crisis. I've had three near death experiences so far this lifetime. I was in a major car accident when Tiera was just six months old. We were returning from a visit to see her father up north when the car we were in had a blowout. The tire popped and the car flipped over twice in a ditch.

The *Saginaw Newspaper* described Tiera as a "miracle baby." She had been asleep in my arms in the back seat when the accident occurred. She was sitting on the side of the road, crying with a single cut on her cheek when the car stopped. I walked away from the scene with an eight-stitch souvenir—four in my forehead and four by my right eye. We were very lucky compared to the injuries endured by several of the other passengers, including Tiera's paternal grandmother, who had to be airlifted via a helicopter to a nearby hospital. Thankfully we all survived.

The second near death experience was an armed robbery. I was held at gun point outside of a strip club on 8 Mile Road in Detroit in the mid-90s. That one left me in shock for several days. I had worked that evening—the gunman must have assumed my earnings were in my backpack. Even with a few drinks in me I was able to think on my feet. "I ain't got no money," I told the mugger, slightly slurring my words. He walked away with about $10 of my money in his pocket.

The thought that the gunman could have blown my brains out that night really rocked my core. It took some time to process. Fortunately no one was physically hurt and what was lost was very little compared to what it could have been.

The third incident happened when Rudy and I were dating (if that's even what you would call our very brief courtship). But none the less, Rudy was there.

If you have to drink or self-medicate to do it, you shouldn't be doing it. That's what I told myself when I first started dancing.

But things changed.

Moreso as the years passed and I found myself *still* working the club scene. It was like a never-ending party, but after some time, *party favors* were helpful to keep the party going. Nothing crazy though, **you had to keep a clear head if you were about making your money.**

By 26, I had been introduced to Ketamine—also known as *Special K*—the drug that was partly to blame for Matthew Perry's death. It made me feel like a dancing fairy goddess gliding with twinkle toes. But it was not to be mixed with anything. I learned that the hard way.

That pivotal night while working at Lace, I snorted some "K" I'd purchased from one of the fellow members of our *Dream Team* (what the DJ called the entertainers of the night shift). When I picture the transaction in my mind, it feels like a scene from the animated classic, *Snow White and the Seven Dwarfs*. The Evil Queen disguised herself as an old hag and presented Snow White a poisoned apple. Except instead of being an old hag, my temptress was a curvaceous goth babe with pale white skin and jet-black hair.

After the hit, I drank champagne with a couple in the VIP room. I knew better than to mix, but I was feeling a little reckless that night—tired of the life I was living, yet I couldn't see a clear path in front of me. I resented the fact that I still relied on dancing to survive. I just wanted to *feel* something different. And as if a genie had granted my wish, the world began to shift in my mind. The walls of the dimly lit room grew even darker. The floor became fluid, and the walls blurred. Something was wrong. I excused myself and stumbled into the bathroom, falling into a stall before becoming trapped in my own mind.

A *"K-hole"* they call it.

Like the movie *The Matrix*, I felt as though I was in a simulated reality.

I was stuck in a maze in my head and in a bathroom stall, all at the same time. I didn't think I would ever get out—EVER! I remember feeling as though I were going to die.

Someone (more than likely a bouncer) removed me from the stall and laid my body on the dressing room floor. I was too far gone to really remember any of it. "Please tell my daughter I love her and that it wasn't her fault." I rambled aloud to anyone that could hear my plea. Even in my altered state I wanted Tiera to know this had nothing to do with her.

I heard the voice of one of the other dancers in the distance, "No! You are going to *stay alive* and tell your daughter you love her yourself!" I have absolutely no clue who that angel was that night, but if this book ever reaches your hands, I thank you from the bottom of my heart.

From that moment on, it was lights out. In the darkness I heard a siren. I saw a flash of light. I felt the cool night air on my skin trying to keep me awake. And then there was nothing.

After some time, I drifted back to consciousness. "Can you get someone to clean her up?" I heard someone call out in the distance. Aside from consciousness, I apparently lost *it* from all possible ends. I recognized the deep tone of Rudy's voice. I woke up in a hospital bed with an IV drip in my arm and a heart rate monitor chirping by my side.

"Hi Kenyatta" a female voice said softly. I looked up to find a woman in a lab coat standing above me with a clipboard in hand. I didn't respond—still a bit dazed and confused. "You're in Nyack Hospital." She paused to see if I would respond. I didn't.

"Do you know why you are here?" I shook my head *yes*. I could now see Rudy standing in the doorway behind her. He wore a mask of concern. She went on. "We were worried about you." She paused again. I said nothing. "You had no neurological responses when they brought you in."

What? I thought. *Is she saying I was brain dead???*

A series of questions proceeded as she took notes in her pad.

What did you take?
How much did you take?
Was it intentional or accidental?
Do you have a history of drug use?
Are you feeling suicidal?

Iron Love | 129

She then asked if I needed counseling, unsure if I was an addict or trying to kill myself—I was neither, but at that moment in my life, I thought death may have been better. She left Rudy and I alone as she proceeded to make her rounds. He slowly walked over to my bedside looking down at me, happy to see me alive, but not happy to see me in my current position. Tears were locked behind his cosmic blue eyes.

Looking up at him, my body weak, my mind still trying to process what happened, I shared, *"I'm going through some shit right now... but if you stay by my side, I can see us having kids together one day",* I predicted our future in that moment. He held my hand. Nothing more was said until I was released. I later learned that Rudy arrived to pick me up from the club at the end of my shift only to find that I wasn't there. One of the bouncers told him about the incident but was unsure where the ambulance had taken me.

Rudy called Good Sam, Westchester Medical and Nyack. He found me at Nyack. I'd never felt so sorry, nor have I ever been so vulnerable, yet in that moment, when Rudy walked over to the bed and I saw his face, I knew he would always be by my side. That was over 25 years ago.

We never really talked about the incident afterwards aside from the vision I shared with him that day. It wasn't something we needed to dissect or analyze. Rudy never judged me—never questioned my worth because of that night. He just stood by me, as steady as always.

His presence alone told me everything I needed to know. He allowed me the space to process what was going on internally—my battle with myself. That's the thing about Iron Love—it doesn't just shine in the easy moments—it shows up in the hardest ones. It stands firm when everything else is crumbling. It doesn't demand perfection; it simply asks for truth, commitment, and for the willingness to stand side by side, supporting each other, even when the road ahead is unclear.

And so, we moved forward together, we built a life, a family, and a love that grew through every season—through heartbreak and healing, through uncertainty and faith, through every challenge that tested us and every joy that reminded us—when we kept choosing each other.

I recently asked Rudy about that time, feeling protective of his younger self. I was trying to understand *why* he didn't walk away after that incident;

unsure of how I would react if either of our sons (or daughter) connected with a love who had some of the same battles I had back then…

"You weren't scared to move forward with a relationship—wondering if this was a pattern of behavior?" The incident took place in July—we'd only just connected at the end of March.

"No", he responded. "I loved you. I always *saw you*." His words brought tears to my eyes. Looking back now, I realize that moment in the hospital wasn't just about survival—it was about rebirth. It was about trusting love, even when I wasn't sure I could trust myself. Because even then, in our weakest state, we saw something worth fighting for.

And now, all these years later, I look at the life we've built—our children, our journey, our unshakable bond—and smile. With each other's love and support, we saw our future… and it was bright and clear.

You're probably thinking, "Wait a minute! Didn't you say it was his decision to go out with someone that got you to open your eyes?" Yes, you are correct. That was the catalyst in the end. My vision of love came first, but because of my *fear,* I tried pushing Rudy away again, even after knowing the truth. *Old limiting beliefs can be hard to break.*

Iron Love isn't about avoiding the pain of the past. It's about taking it head on, learning from it, growing stronger from it. It's about seeing clearly, even when fear tries to cloud the truth. Rudy's steady presence, his unwavering belief in me—in us was a mirror reflecting back the love I had always deserved but wasn't sure I could trust. And in the end, it wasn't just his decision to stay that changed everything—it was my decision to finally believe—to let go of fear and embrace the love that had been there all along.

Iron Love doesn't waiver. It doesn't bend under pressure. It simply endures. And so, through every test, every moment of doubt, and every leap of faith, we found our way—together.

LIFE AFTER LOVE

Miss Me

When I come to the end of the road

And the sun has set for me

I want no rites in a gloom-filled room

Why cry for a soul set free?

Miss me...a little, But not too long and not

With your head bowed low.

Remember the love that we once shared

Miss me... But let me go

For this is a journey that we all must take

And each must go alone

It's all a part of the master's plan

A step on the road to home.

When you are lonely and sick at heart

Go to the friends we know

And bury your sorrow in doing good deeds

Miss me... But let me go

AUTHOR UNKNOWN

We come to understand the journey through this world is unpredictable. And with all of its beauty and moments of joy, there are situations and events beyond our control—some expected, others unforeseen.

Death.

An inevitable part of life, one we will all come to experience from one side—and the other. But sometimes, it arrives without a warning. No one is ever truly prepared for the loss of a loved one, and when it comes too soon...

It's been just about two years since I witnessed the most beautiful young love take root. Marie and Thomas had just declared their love and commitment to one another before a small gathering of close family and friends. Their ceremony took place in the beautiful courtyard of their newly renovated fairytale dream home—a perfect beginning to their forever.

Their connection was like magic, an energy that filled every room they entered. It was pure electric. Anyone who witnessed their love could feel it and was excited to see what their future would hold, but in less than a year after exchanging their vows, it was gone. Their whole world was shattered in an instant. A tragic, untimely accident extinguished their love's light in mere seconds.

"Till death do us part." Thomas was gone, leaving Marie with a broken heart and a lifetime of dreams that would go unfulfilled.

Grief—it's complex. No two people experience it quite the same way. My dear Marie is still in the thick of it and we as a community continue to lift her up until she feels strong enough to stand on her own.

Thomas would have wanted her to keep *living,* to continue to dream big even in his absence. But healing for everyone comes in its own time. Witnessing such heartbreak up close led me to seek out stories of others who have found the strength to carry on after loss. This journey led me to a former neighbor, Bob Bennett. Bob and his wife, Coleen, shared a beautiful marriage—over 15 years of love and partnership. But before Coleen, there was Fran. Bob and his past love, Fran spent many wonderful years together before she passed.

"I was blessed with Fran, my love from college—married 24 years and raised our three amazing children", Bob shared. "My wife Fran was athletic, young, no vices, and lit up any room she entered. She got breast cancer and fought valiantly but ultimately succumbed. She would say 'why not me?' I won't begin to tell you the alternative and standard cancer treatments she went through."

Bob continued, "She, like Rudy, was a teacher and then an administrator—she really did change many, many lives in her tenure. Just an amazing lady. That's why after she passed, we wanted to continue her good work with special education high school seniors. Education was her passion."

Bob and his family created the **FAB For Life Foundation** in Fran's honor. FAB for Life is a nonprofit 501(c)(3) organization established in November 2007 with the mission to aid graduating special education students with post-graduate costs associated with continuing education and career training programs.

Some years later, Bob met and fell in love with Coleen, "an amazing woman whose passion was working with babies and children—many autistic, or developmentally delayed. Coleen was raising her children pretty much as a single parent—another beautiful soul who lights up a room. Coleen is the most selfless, humble person in the world! I am truly blessed—why I have had such good fortune is beyond belief."

And while Bob found love again, he and the family still held space in their lives for their beloved Fran, who was taken way too soon. An April 4, 2023 post on Bob's Facebook page along with photos reads:

Happy Birthday Fran in Heaven! You are always within us. Thank you for all of your love, showing us the way to lead our lives with direct passion and love. Always within all of us.

Bob passed seventeen months after sharing his story of life after love with me for this chapter. And now his beloved Coleen is left to continue life without his physical presence. I recently FaceTimed Coleen to catch up. We hadn't connected since shortly after Bob's funeral. I wanted to get her permission to use Bob's name in order to share *FAB for Life* in this chapter. It was so awesome to reconnect. At some point during the conversation, I asked if she'd *received any signs* from Bob of his continued existence since his passing.

"You know, it's funny you should ask me that…" She lit up as she spoke. "I was down in Florida a few weeks ago visiting a girlfriend, and she asked me the same thing. I told her I *wanted* to believe, but I just wasn't sure if he'd send me any signs." Coleen thought that since Bob was now in spirit form, he might be back with his beloved Fran. She couldn't *see* there being enough room for her too.

At that moment questions flooded my head as if not from myself:

"Do you believe in God or a higher power?"

"Yes." She responded.

"Do you believe this source loves us all?"

Another acknowledgement followed.

The impression I received—the message in my mind—was that Bob's spirit now exists much like that of the Universe itself: no longer confined to a human shell. His love; no longer bound by the measures of this world. Time and space has become infinite. "You can feel his love and presence here, even if he is no longer with us in physical form. His love can be felt by more than one simultaneously." The words just came to me.

Coleen spoke up, "But I did recently have an experience that made me raise an eyebrow and kind of turn my head sideways." I leaned in to hear more. Coleen reached into her pocket to retrieve an item as she continued. "I had no expectations about seeing any signs. Totally shut down the idea that I would experience anything at all like that." She pulled her hand out of her pocket and opened her hand, exposing the tiniest red cardinal figurine. She held it up to the camera.

"This little gift from my neighbors made me consider it *could be* some kind of sign." There was a moment of silence between us before she continued. "I walk a few miles every day and would see cardinals on the trail but a few days ago when I was returning from my stroll—there was a red cardinal in the bush near the bridge I cross to get home. I stopped and looked at it for a minute, and then out popped another one! I thought it may be a sign but then questioned it."

There are no coincidences.

It was around that moment Coleen looked up. You could see a twinkle in her eyes. "Wow!" she exclaimed. "Ok, I didn't really notice this before, but I have to show you." She stood up and walked into the living room, phone in hand.

"So, a few years ago while Bob and I were away on vacation, I saw this painting I loved—it had beautiful rock formations with flowers around it. Bob loved it too. He turned to the guy selling it and said, *'My wife loves this painting.'* and he bought it." She then rotated the camera to face the canvas mounted on her living room wall. In the top left corner of the painting, resting on a rock, partly covered by ferns was a full chested red cardinal.

"I love it! It seems Bob may have just picked the cardinal as a sign for you." My heart was full. We conversed about signs and synchronicities for a few hours. I shared what I've experienced since reading *Signs: The Secret Language of the Universe* by Laura Lynne Jackson. It was a wonderful, eye-opening afternoon.

In a 2019 *CBS News* segment promoting her work, Laura shares, "People who cross are really still with us to connect and feel love from. When we open our mind and heart we can open up to a whole new language."

Laura teaches that our loved ones use default signs to communicate with us after crossing. Some of the popular ones include coins in our path, electronic disturbances, birds, butterflies, dragonflies, meaningful songs, and specific number sequences.

You can also ask your loved ones for specific signs to show you. Right about now, I know you're thinking, *This book just took a turn.* But I promise you, I learned this connection to be real and true a few years ago, after asking my dad to show me *lions* as a sign of his continued presence. He crossed when I was 21. At first, I thought for sure the signs I received had to be coincidental but after attending Laura's workshop, *An Illuminated Life* at the Omega Institute in Rhinebeck, NY, in 2023, my world completely changed.

The workshop drew over 430 attendees traveling from nine countries and 44 states. I call the event a cross between grief counseling and wizard camp; you attended because you see things/feel things (that are not seen or experienced by most) and want to learn more about it, or you lost someone you wanted to connect with. I considered myself a hybrid—I'd received signs and also lost loved ones I was open to connecting with. If you were in attendance that weekend, it was clear you were meant to be there. My dear friend Michele Phillips planned to meet me at Omega. She was traveling from Long Island and hadn't yet arrived.

I got there in no time and decided to explore the grounds. I discovered the Omega Café and decided to see if they had ice cream. Why I was craving a frozen dessert was beyond me. It was a fairly cold October afternoon. I accomplished my mission, finding pistachio ice cream at the Café. Yum! I decided to take it and sit outside.

It was drizzling, but nothing crazy. There were people sprinkled all along the deck, but I was drawn to sit next to one person in particular. Sitting alone taking in the sound of the nearby rushing stream was a woman around my age. She had dark hair, deep eyes and a welcoming smile.

I asked if I could sit with her. We introduced ourselves and engaged in light conversation. Her name was Cindy. We soon discovered we are the same age, and she shares a birthday with my daughter, August 3rd. "That makes you a Leo," I said out loud, though at that moment it didn't register that there was a *lion* connection.

During our exchange, she asked why I was there. I shared how I came to know Laura Lynne's book and that *I believed* my biological father's mom, who passed away a few years prior, facilitated (from the other side) for me to find out the truth about my dad—that he wasn't my biological father. It's just the way I found out; the way things unfolded… the timeliness and synchronistic nature of it all… it just seemed to be very *otherworldly*.

Cindy turned to me and asked, "Are you sure it wasn't your dad that passed?" I was puzzled, though at the same time realizing as he had crossed, he would know the truth. I stopped mid-lick and looked at Cindy while pulling the ice cream from my lips.

Cindy went on, "Was your dad bald?" she asked.

"Yes," I responded.

"Was his name Harry?"

My eyes widened. "Harold!" I exclaimed.

It was evident that she took me by surprise with her questions. "I'm sorry. I should have told you—I'm a medium. Your dad has been trying to get through to you ever since you sat next to me," she shared. "He just wants you to know that it was *him* who facilitated for you to find out the truth, *not* your grandma."

It was a lot to process before the workshop even began. Now to be perfectly clear, I shared no more than my name, my daughter's birthdate, my age, and my theories about my bio-dad's mom. Nothing more.

Cindy went on to describe the outfit my dad is wearing in my most memorable photo with him. Before we parted ways, Cindy delivered another message she said was from my dad. "He says to *keep your eyes open*—he's going to send you more signs this weekend."

Over the course of the next few days, I received many signs, and not just from my dad. The mic drop though, was on the last day of the workshop. The moment came when I would meet Laura Lynne Jackson herself. It was when I snapped a photo of her with my girlfriend, Michele, that I noticed a stunning gold ring on her finger. I asked if I could see it. I lifted her hand in the palm of mine and there it was—a gold lion head with a clear quartz crystal in its mouth. I burst into tears.

My dad showed me a lion on the author's finger. You can't make this up! I was extremely emotional, and it showed. The picture I took with Laura was horrible! I couldn't post it on social media. I had to have a redo. So I took a number and got back in line. The queue was now wrapping around the interior of the hall. Luckily, I was number 19.

As I waited my turn, I shared the story of what just happened with two women standing next to me. The one closest to me looked me in the eyes and said, "My name actually means *Eternal Lion* in my language." At that very moment, my phone *dinged*. It was my father-in-law, but in my phone, he is listed as *Daddy*.

The message read:

Daddy *"I'm still working on your signs, what do you think..."*

My father-in-law had been working on a directional sign for me for our cabin in Michigan, but the timeliness (that he had sent it right then, though we hadn't spoken in two weeks) and the way the message read…

꘎

Ever since that weekend at Omega, I've been seeing signs from loved ones passed and discovering new connections and ways of communicating. It's as though the event truly illuminated my life—there is no way anyone can tell me that *death* is the end. But as with everything in life, some people may not believe or may not be ready to accept this reality. And that's ok. We all come to it when we're supposed to.

As shared in *Coping with Grief and Loss: Stages of Grief, the Grieving Process, and Learning to Heal* by Melinda Smith, M.A., Lawrence Robinson and Jeanne Segal, Ph.D published on Helpguide.org, *"Grieving is a highly individual experience; there's no right or wrong way to grieve. How you grieve depends on many factors, including your personality and coping style, your life experience, your faith and how significant the loss was to you. Healing happens gradually; It can't be forced or hurried—and there is no "normal" timetable for grieving."*

While grieving a loss is an inevitable part of life, there are ways to help cope with the pain, come to terms with your grief, and eventually, find a way to pick up the pieces and move forward with your life.

- **Allow yourself the time you need to process.** The pain is yours and it's ok to let it go when you're ready.

- **Tap into others who have experienced similar loss.** There is something comforting about not having to explain your grief—they get it. Connecting with individuals or support groups can be helpful in not feeling alone.

- **Talk about your love**—share pictures, stories, and videos. Our loved ones live on through our memories.

- **Find ways to remember them**— plant a butterfly bush or a tree in their honor. I've even noted the idea of having a teddy bear or blanket made from some of their favorite clothes.

- **Travel**—visit a friend or even consider going somewhere alone. Sometimes getting away and experiencing unfamiliar environments, meeting new people can help with processing emotions and giving space for new perspectives and getting away from the constant daily reminders.

- **Turn your pain into purpose.** My girlfriend Ziggy created the *Swim for Yinka Foundation* in honor of her late husband who passed after an accidental drowning. Paying it forward can aid with healing—turning the pain of grief into something meaningful and assisting others in the process.
- **And if nothing else resonates, find a grief counselor.** Sometimes it is just too much to process alone and as much as our loved ones want to support us, they aren't always equipped with the proper tools.

Wherever you are in the grieving process, know that right here and now, I am sending you so much light, love, and positive energy. And no matter how heavy the weight—you are not alone.

Death is not the end of love.

Death is an evolution in the way we experience love. The pain of losing a loved one is felt deeply, as the love we once gave and received is no longer exchanged in the ways we've always known and communicated it. As shared earlier in our journey together, with learning anything new, there is often confusion before clarity sets in. And in this case, the confusion is felt as pain—the ache of not being able to touch, or share space with your love the way you once had.

But when you are ready, should you choose to stay open to the possibility that they are ever-present in your life, you may begin to feel their love in a new way. You may find your cardinal. Your lion. Your Sign.

And just as one chapter ends, so shall it begin…

Loving you.

A New Beginning

I recently visited with my 84-year young friend, Rose, in Detroit. We sat and drank tea at her house while I was in town visiting my mom. Rose has a colorful personality and a very youthful spirit—she kind of reminds me of the character, Ninny Threadgoode from the 1991 classic *Fried Green Tomatoes*.

As we sat in her kitchen that afternoon, I began to think about her late husband, George. He succumbed to esophageal cancer 15 years prior. I proposed the same question to Rose that I had to Coleen, curious as to whether George has tried to communicate with her at all since he passed.

"Oh! dear God, please no!" She laughed, almost losing her tea as she maintained eye contact with me. I hadn't anticipated her response.

"I'm so happy with my life now. Please let him stay in heaven where he belongs!"

Rose and George married when she was just 21. They were together for 48 years. "It was hell!" she shared.

"If I had to do it all over again, I would run the other way!", she chuckled, making fun though she meant every word. George, from what she shared, wasn't physically abusive, but he didn't *fill her cup* in any way.

Can you imagine spending nearly half your life with someone not being happy? No, don't! Don't even put the idea in your head. We no longer live in a time when people (especially women) are confined to a relationship out of necessity. Not too long ago societal norms, legal restrictions, and financial dependency created invisible chains that made leaving nearly impossible. Marriage was seen not just as a union of love, but as a *duty*—a role to fulfill, even when the emotional core had long gone hollow.

"Divorce wasn't an option," Rose declared, stirring honey into her second cup. "I didn't believe in it." She took a stance as to why she didn't leave, though the marriage was totally loveless. "Besides, my parents lived in a trailer up in the UP (Upper Peninsula). I knew I couldn't go back home."

Today, we live in an era of choices, limited only by the mental restraints we put on ourselves.

- *I can't afford to leave.*
- *I have no place to go.*

- *My partner needs me.*
- *Marriage is supposed to be hard.*
- *No one else will want me.*
- *It's not all bad—we have some good moments.*
- *What will people think?*
- ***I don't want to hurt the kids*** (meanwhile staying in a dysfunctional relationship can do more long-term damage than leaving).

If you can believe it, you can achieve it.

I can't remember how young I was the first time I heard those words, though I know it was in elementary school. I believed in love and happiness, so I never gave up. Believe me now, as I share these words with you: Know that you weren't put on this planet to be unhappy. You traveled here to learn and experience love—true love. Manifest it, recognize it, accept it, build it up and hold on to it. There is nothing like experiencing a life of Iron Love.

STAYING IN LOVE

The Slow Death

One of my dearest friends recently messaged me a public Instagram text carousel post shared from the profile **@Iamadoria**. It was dated **February 23rd** and featured a background photo of a young couple smiling in an embrace, with the husband lifting and holding his wife midair.

The messages instantly brought tears to my eyes:

- ***What if you woke up tomorrow and your spouse was gone**? Really sit with that for a second. Not just gone for the day. Not just in the next room. But gone. No more texts. No more "What's for dinner?" No more body next to yours at night.*
- ***Too many marriages die slowly***, *not from one big mistake, but from a thousand small moments of neglect.*
- ***You stop saying "I love you" with meaning***. *You stop touching them just because. You stop trying because you assume they'll always be there.*
- ***And one day, you realize...****they don't look at you the same. The spark you thought would last forever? Gone. Not because you stopped loving each other, but because you stopped choosing each other.*
- ***So, before you go another day treating your spouse like a given, ask yourself***: *If today was the last day you had with them... would they know, without a doubt, how deeply they were loved?*
- ***Because one day... that last chance will be real***. *And you don't want to look back wishing you would have loved them better.*

As you may have come to realize already along this reading journey, manifesting and accepting love is just the beginning. Think about our attention spans as humans—one minute, we're all about the keto diet, the next, we're swearing by intermittent fasting. The same principle applies to relationships. You have to keep living, evolving, and spicing things up to prevent stagnation. Otherwise you run the risk of becoming a modern version of *All in the Family*. (Oh, I know a few of you will have to look that one up.)

We all have friends who have experienced the slow death of a relationship—it happens gradually. But with a conscious decision to keep choosing each other every day, love will inevitably grow stronger. As I shared in *Trusting Love*, it was around year 13 that Rudy and I really started shaking things up. We became the best dance partners… figuratively. My Rudy still does a chicken dance or stands in the center as I dance around him making him look good.

Love, like bodybuilding, isn't just about showing up—it's about putting in the work, day after day, rep after rep. It's about breaking down, rebuilding, and coming back stronger. From the very beginning, Rudy and I trained for this partnership, even before we realized we were in it for the long haul. Our love story wasn't one of instant clarity; it was about conditioning—strengthening our bond, testing our endurance, and discovering how far we could push ourselves together.

"Being married to Kenyatta is exhausting," Rudy teased at R2M's 10th Anniversary celebration. Yes, like a coach, I push us, and Rudy's a willing and active participant, running up and down the obstacle course of life together, hand in hand.

We've faced challenging moments—the kind that could take you out of the game. Starting with being able to accept his love, my near-death experience, the uncovering of secrets, our daughter's cancer scare… It all tested our mental, emotional, and spiritual endurance. These weren't just obstacles; they were heavyweights life threw on the bar, and we had to dig deep to lift them. But we did—spotting each other when the weight got too heavy, pushing through, and finding strength in the struggle.

Trust, like muscle, takes time to build and seconds to tear. The challenges we faced—like the moments of broken trust—were setbacks, but setbacks aren't the end. Just as a torn muscle rebuilds stronger after proper training, so did our commitment to each other. We put in the rehab work, reinforcing our foundation, improving our form, and making sure we stayed aligned.

Love, like training, can't just be about the grind through the reps—you have to enjoy the process too. Rudy and I realized that our love and life had to be more than just existing. After I confessed to Rudy my need for a *dance partner*, we intentionally incorporated more fun into our lives and everything else started to flow. And listen, though we love traveling together, that hasn't always been an option. But we've always found ways to connect—whether it's preparing a meal together, taking a nice long walk or hike, and dancing… even if it's just in our own living room alone.

And through it all, we never stop supporting each other's growth—in the gym, with our careers, personally—we understand that one partner's strength doesn't diminish the other; it elevates both. We've been each other's coach, training partner, and motivator, knowing that success isn't about outpacing each other. Success is about spotting each other—encouraging and celebrating the progress we make together.

Communication is our core strength, the stabilizer that keeps everything balanced. We learned that love isn't just about being strong individually—it's about being strong together. Together, we're still training, still growing, still adding weight, testing limits, and building endurance. And just like bodybuilding, love isn't about perfection—it's about the commitment to keep showing up. No shortcuts. No skipping reps. No easy way out.

Only *Iron Love.*

~

I hope this journey helps you create a love that makes you want to live, experience, and adventure together in ways that fulfills each of you. My sole reason for sharing *Iron Love* is to help others build and sustain a love that stays strong, flexible, and enduring, just like a well-conditioned body. No matter what stage of love you're in, with resilience, faith, and a willingness to grow, you can create a life of love and fulfillment—one you may have only dreamed of.

It *does* exist. And it can be yours. Just always remember: The most important love of all is **self-love**. When you nurture that, all other love can flow.

Thank you for embarking on this journey with me.

I look forward to hearing your **stories of love** as *Iron Love* gains strength and muscle memory, creating a foundation that lasts a lifetime.

I Love You.

♥

ACKNOWLEDGEMENTS

This book was made possible by the many cast members who helped shape me into who I am today. Thank you for the role you played no matter how big or small.

Without the part you played, *Iron Love* wouldn't exist.

Rudy Thomas Arietta—My Iron Love. Thank you for always seeing me, even when I wasn't sure I could see myself. You are my rock, my anchor, my love, life partner, and my best friend. I appreciate you more than words can say and look forward to the next phase of our lives together. *Happy 25th Anniversary!*

Tiera Rice-Royo—My amazing and talented daughter, publisher and web designer (who knew?) Thank you for being my life motivator. For you, I pushed. From you, I learned. Loving you every step of the way. When I had the vision of my publisher, I knew it would have a lion and wings, but who would have thought it would be my Leo daughter and her company named after one of our guardian angels. There couldn't be anything more perfect. I am so excited to be giving birth to this work with you holding my hand, coaching me along as I push. We did this together.

Rudy Harold—My son. Thank you for being you—Solid like the mountains you climb, as easygoing as the streams you fish, and warm like the breads you bake. You inspire me.

Sean Robert—Mirror of my soul. Thank you for being my teacher. And never forget how awesome you are. Looking forward to having you record one of (if not all of) my audiobooks.

Raevyn, Elisa, Ayden and Little Luis—Your futures are as bright as your smiles. A publicist once told me to write what I want my grandchildren to know. May *Iron Love* be a guide to help you navigate your lives and love as you travel this wonderful land. Nana loves you and will always be here for you.

Roberta Jones (Mom)—It's like making a soup… change one ingredient, and you change the dish. I love who I am, and I am grateful for your contribution to this *nutty stew*. Thank you for loving me, for the sacrifices you made to give us a better life, and for helping me see the love I wasn't yet ready to accept. Most of all, thank you for growing with us as we've grown.

Julius Smith (Uncle Boot) & Harry Smith (Uncle Harry)—Thank you for being the men I needed in my life. Your roles have played a significant part in my becoming.

Joan Leavey (aka Ma)—You single handedly raised the most amazing human being (with the support of your tribe). Thank you for everything that you've instilled in him and for always being there to support us and our family in any way possible.

Rudy Arietta (aka Daddy)—Thank you for being one of our biggest cheerleaders and for the fabulous cardinals and signs.

To our dear friends, the Bournes, the Cabraies and the Kahns—Thank you for being a part of our journey. Our lives wouldn't be the same without you in it.

My Positivity Posse—Patricia Zariello, Michele Phillips and Patricia Stark—Thank you for all the love and support you've given me throughout this journey, both in front and behind the scenes. Looking forward to our next slumber party.

Donna Hendricks Moore & Cinthujaa Sivanantha-Samuel—Your contributions to this journey are beyond measure. The introductions to John Assaraf and Laura Lynne Jackson opened me in ways none of us could have anticipated… the gifts that keep on giving. Thank you.

Coleen Bennett & Zewditu Mulugeta—Thank you for sharing your love.

Brenda MacLeish—Who knew that a closet design could turn into your daughter being my editor. It was always meant to be. <3

Jessica MacLeish—My Editor. Your guidance helped shape *Iron Love* into what it was meant to be. Thank you for seeing the vision, for asking the right questions. Your quiet presence left a lasting imprint.

Jocelyn Jane Cox—My Writing Coach—Thank you for pulling me ashore whilst I swam through a sea of words and thoughts. *Iron Love* would not have come to life without you. Looking forward to our next adventure.

My R2M Realty Family—I could not have done *Iron Love* without you. Thank you for allowing me the space to get this project out and holding down the fort when I needed to write. I love you all and hope that you are proud of this work. And my assistants, Nakisha Carter & Patricia Zariello, thank you for learning how to read *Kenyatta*. So not an easy thing to do but you manage patiently. ;-)

My Rockland County Community—Thank you for embracing me and allowing me space to heal, grow and give in the best ways possible.

My Goldman Sachs 10KSB Cohort 41 Family—You inspire me to continue to grow. Looking forward to celebrating with you.

My OHS Family—Osborn Knights forever! Thank you for your lifetime of friendship and support.

Thank you to God, The Universe, my guardian angels and loved ones who have crossed, forever lighting and opening my path. I know without your guidance, none of this would have been possible.

I love you.

♥

KENYATTA JONES-ARIETTA is a visionary, storyteller, and entrepreneur whose journey has been anything but ordinary. From teen mom and exotic dancer to successful real estate broker, Kenyatta is living proof that love, intention, and resilience can reshape a life. She is the founder of R2M Realty, Inc.®, a multi-state real estate brokerage known for heart- centered service, and co-creator of River & Creek, a boutique vacation rental brand.

In Iron Love, her debut memoir and growth guide, Kenyatta shares deeply personal stories and lessons about choosing love—in all its forms—through the highs, lows, and in-betweens of life. With a voice that's raw, wise, and unfiltered, she invites readers to reflect, heal, and rise.

Kenyatta lives in New York with her husband of 25 years, Rudy, their Great Dane Bruce, and a family that inspires every chapter.

Kenyattaarietta.com IronLoveBook.com

Instagram: @kenyattar2M.com

Linkedin.com/in/kenyatta-jones-arietta-94624056

Photo taken by Yadira Lopez

Eula Rae Printing and Publishing, an imprint of Depending on The Day, LLC., was founded in 2015 in Rockland County, NY by Tiera Rice—a passionate writer, speaker, and creative visionary. The name is a tribute to two remarkable people: "Eula," Tiera's great-grandmother, whose legacy of gentleness, strength, and love lives on through stories passed down by family; and "Rae," honoring Tiera's firstborn daughter Raevyn, who gave her a reason to rise and reclaim her life's purpose.

Eula Rae was born from the belief that stories, especially those often overlooked, have the power to transform, connect, and heal. With a deep commitment to authenticity, creative freedom, and soulful expression, the company champions voices from all walks of life. Whether fiction or nonfiction, every book published through Eula Rae carries a piece of someone's truth, beauty, and legacy.

As a proud, independent press, Eula Rae Printing and Publishing stands for more than books. It stands for reclaiming your voice, owning your story, and daring to share it with the world.

To learn more or connect, visit: www.eularae.com